POETS OF THE TWENTIES:
100 GREAT POEMS

BOOKS BY CHARD POWERS SMITH

POETRY
Along the Wind
Lost Address
The Quest of Pan
Hamilton: A Poetic Drama
Prelude to Man

ABOUT POETRY
Pattern and Variation in Poetry
ABOUT POETS
Annals of the Poets

NOVELS
Artillery of Time
Ladies Day
Turn of the Dial
He's in the Artillery Now

HISTORY
The Housatonic (Rivers of America)
Yankees and God

BIOGRAPHY
Where the Light Falls: A Portrait of
Edwin Arlington Robinson

POETS *of the* TWENTIES:
100 Great Poems

Edited by Chard Powers Smith

Foreword by Peter Viereck

CLARK McCUTCHEON

Port Washington, New York

Acknowledgments and thanks are due the following for their permission to reprint poems:

JAMES BENÉT for *Whale* by William Rose Benét.

BRANDT AND BRANDT for the lines from *John Brown's Body* by Stephen Vincent Benét (Holt, Rinehart & Winston Inc.) Copyright 1927, 1928 by Stephen Vincent Benét. Copyright renewed 1955, 1956 by Rosemary Carr Benét.

CHATTO & WINDUS LTD. for *Nelly Trim* (from *The Espalier* by Sylvia Townsend Warner, Copyright 1925).

COWARD–MC CANN INC. for *Honeysuckle* and *Mercy By Night* (from *Poems and Portraits*, Copyright 1940 by Christopher La Farge.)

BABETTE DEUTSCH for the lines from *Epistle to Prometheus*, Copyright 1931.

NORMA MILLAY ELLIS for the poems by Edna St. Vincent Millay from her *Collected Poems* (Harper & Row) Copyright 1923, 1928, 1931, 1951, 1955, 1958 by Edna St. Vincent Millay and Norma Millay Ellis.

HILDEGARD FLANNER for *Driving Clock*, Copyright 1942.

FUNK & WAGNALLS for *Thought's End*, Copyright 1954 (from *Poems; A Selection* by Leonie Adams).

HARCOURT, BRACE & WORLD, INC. for *The Dry Salvages* (from *Four Quartets*, Copyright 1943 by T. S. Eliot) and *Impressions, IV, Actualities, I,* and *Realities, II,* Copyright 1923, 1951 by E. E. Cummings (reprinted from his volume *Poems 1923-1954*).

HILL & WANG, INC. for the sonnets from *Collected And New Poems 1924-1963*, Copyright © 1963 by Mark Van Doren.

HOLT, RINEHART, & WINSTON INC. for *The Poet* from *Selected Poems* by Raymond Holden, Copyright 1946 by Holt, Rinehart, & Winston, Inc., for the lines from *Lincoln* from *Selected Poems* by John Gould Fletcher, Copyright © 1966 by Charlie May Fletcher, for the lines from *Chorus for Survival* in *Collected Poems* by Horace Gregory, Copyright 1941 © 1964 by Horace Gregory, for *The Shape of Memory, Notes On The Mystery, Cruciform,* and *Torch* from *The Shape of Memory* by Winifred Welles, Copyright 1944 by Holt, Rinehart, & Winston, Inc., and for *The Sound of Trees, West-Running Brook, Once By The Pacific, All Revelation, Stopping By Woods On A Snowy Evening, Bereft, I Could Give All To Time,* and the lines from *I Will Sing You One-O*—all from *The Complete Poems of Robert Frost*, Copyright 1916, 1923, 1928, by Holt, Rinehart, & Winston, Inc., Copyright 1942, 1944, 1951, © 1956 by Robert Frost.

HOUGHTON MIFFLIN COMPANY for *You, Andrew Marvell* and *Epistle To Be Left In The Earth* from *Collected Poems* by Archibald MacLeish and for *Patterns* from *Complete Poetical Works* by Amy Lowell.

LIVERIGHT PUBLISHING CORPORATION for the lines from *Proem: To Brooklyn Bridge* and *Cape Hatteras* (both from *The Bridge* in *The Collected Poems of Hart Crane*, Copyright © renewed 1961 by Liveright Publishing Corporation.

THE MACMILLAN COMPANY for *Mr. Flood's Party* and the lines from *Rembrandt To Rembrandt*, Copyright 1921 by Edwin Arlington Robinson, Copyright renewed 1949 by Ruth Nivison, for *Karma, As It Looked Then,* and *A Christmas Sonnet*, Copyright 1925 by Edwin Arlington Robinson, Copyright renewed 1952 by Ruth Nivison and Barbara R. Holt, for the lines from *Tristram*, Copyright 1927 by Edwin Arlington Robinson, Copyright renewed 1955 by Ruth Nivison and Barbara R. Holt, for the lines from *The Three Taverns*, Copyright 1920 by

To Kendall

❀ *To my wife, Eunice Clark Smith, I am grateful for the exacting work of reading the text in progress and making innumerable corrections which have improved it, both in detail and in the large. To my friends Winifred Rorty, Lea Ehrich, Charles M. Fair, Harry Staley and Arthur N. Collins, I am grateful for definitive advice in cases where I was doubtful about inclusions and exclusions of particular poems.*

❀ FOREWORD

This anthology is an attempt to revive interest in an important period of American poetry, the 1920's. The attempt succeeds. It does so both on the level of pleasing and on the level of instructing. Thereby it commends itself both to the general reader and to the student.

Chard Powers Smith is well qualified as editor. For at least three reasons. First, he was particularly active in the 1920's with his own excellent books of poetry. Second, he knew personally almost every name here published and criticized, especially Robinson, Gregory, Mark Van Doren, the Benéts, Elinor Wylie, Robinson Jeffers. Third, his 1932 volume (soon to be revised), *Pattern and Variation in Poetry*, being in some ways the most comprehensive treatise ever written on the subject, has prepared him for the illuminating critical commentaries that pull together each section of poems.

In mathematics it has long been recognized that a non-Euclidian geometry will sometimes serve functions as important as those of the Euclidian main line. In modern poetry today, the recognized main line is the revolt against the 19th century that began around 1912 and, of course, included the Imagists, Pound, and Eliot. The present book is important—and usefully controversial—as the non-Euclidian geometry of the muses. Although rightly also including samples of the great and beautiful work of Eliot and the main line, the bulk of the book consists of poets who rejected what today is taught as 1912, who never broke with the 19th century. At their best, they developed the 19th century (not blindly imitated it, no tedious Victorian late romanticism,* but developed it) into the new and more machine-ridden context of the 1920's. Don't look now, but much of today's so-called main line may turn out to be a dowdy

* What Mario Praz brilliantly called "the romantic agony" aged into the rheumatic agony.

outer suburb in the future. Meanwhile, Mr. Smith's non-Euclidians may turn out to be poetry's central geometry after all, once a new generation of readers realizes the absurdity of such modernist dicta as, for example, "iambic pentameter is dead."

Nevertheless these poets of the losing side became neglected or totally forgotten. The average English department student of today will never have read them; nor—as many are out of print—will he be able to read them even if he learns of their names. Yet he may find in them, as he leafs these pages, a lost and resurrected loveliness. This fact justifies class-room use of the book and makes it a unique, absolutely unique introduction to America's literary past. Here is a list of included poets who either are completely out of print or else (especially Jeffers and Masters) are out of print with the book from which some extremely long and important excerpt is here included; William Rose Benét, Anna Hempstead Branch, Christopher La Farge, Hildegarde Flanner, John Gould Fletcher, Raymond Holden, Robinson Jeffers, Edgar Lee Masters, James Rorty, George Santayana, Chard Powers Smith, Sylvia Townsend Warner, Winifred Welles, Babette Deutsch, and Horace Gregory (whose *Chorus For Survival* is recalled, in part, from an earlier out-of-print version).

Let us conclude (poetry being so personal) with a personal note. Last January, *prior* to seeing or knowing of the present anthology, I received from Bobbs-Merrill, my New York publisher, the galleys of my *New and Selected Poems*, scheduled for September, 1967. A friend, helping me read my proofs, remarked:

> "Though your own work is of the 1940's through '60's, your particular music echoes the 20's. Which poems of approximately the 20's have most influenced your rhythms?"

I replied:

> "Robinson's *Luke Havergal*, Frost's *Stopping By Woods On A Snowy Evening*, and Hart Crane's *Proem: To Brooklyn Bridge*."

Soon after, I received Mr. Smith's manuscript in the mail, with a request for my reaction. The enthusiasm of my above reaction, which I trust is objective as much as subjective, is not wholly irrelevant to the fact that the three opening poems of the anthology are precisely the three named above.

The odds against such a triple coincidence are astronomical. What does it mean? What kind of sorcerer is Chard Powers Smith?

Peter Viereck
Mt. Holyoke College, S. Hadley, Mass.
March, 1967

❀ CONTENTS

DEATH

MYSTICAL REALIZATION

BIBLIOGRAPHY

❀ PREFACE

The aim of this book is to present the major work of the Ameri-
can poets of the twenties. This body of verse comprises a unique
collection integrated around the quest for truth on the part of
The Lost Generation which had repudiated the truth to which it
was born. Furthermore, it is my aim to proclaim the poetic outburst
of the twenties—more specifically, of the period between the First
World War and the Great Depression—not only as the first significant one in America, but also as qualified to take a place on the shelf
of history alongside the poetic records of the Elizabethan, English
Augustan, and English Romantic Ages. I would like to assert that a
few generations hence, though fashion may have turned against the
romantic exuberance of this movement, yet it will be recognized,
even by critics and teachers who dislike it personally, as a significant, permanent contribution to literary history.

Since the ascendance of the New Criticism in the late thirties, one
of the fallacies it has imposed upon the English curricula in the col-
leges has been the dating of Modern American Poetry from the
appearance of Eliot's *The Waste Land* in 1922. That is indeed a fair
date for the earliest recognition of that semi-classicism which the
New Criticism promoted. Yet for another decade both the New
Criticism and its poetical reflection remained no more than an *avant
garde* eddying along two successive dominant currents. Of permanent importance was the neo-romantic movement whose principal
work is the subject of this book and whose revolt, beginning in the
1890's, against late nineteenth-century pseudo-romanticism, was
the real beginning of modern American poetry. This revolt was
successful by 1912, and it remained dominant until the early thirties. Being signalized by passionate, self-expressive individualism, it
was consciously a school only in the sense that all of its subdivisions
addressed the common enemy, Victorian sentimentality. Following

it, the evanescent school of Social Consciousness spoke for the left-
ist tendency of the depressed early and mid-thirties, and by repudi-
ating emotional romanticism for reason, prepared the way for semi-
classicism. The latter school, important for its critical prose rather
than its verse, came into authority in the late thirties, remained so
till the early fifties, and has left academic, New Critical prejudices
to this day. A fourth modern school, probably evanescent, was that
of Colloquialism which repudiated the esoteric elegance of the semi-
classicals and, with the Beatniks for spearhead, performed through
the fifties. In the sixties our poetry seems to be passing into a new
phase under the leadership of poets who began to be heard in the
fifties. They look askance both at their contemporaries the Colloquials and at their parents the New Critics with their semi-
classicism. And they look at least curiously at their grandparents
and their resounding flood of neo-romanticism in the twenties.

The chief qualities of late nineteenth-century poetry, which we
are pleased to blame on the British by calling it Victorian, were
stereotyped emotions, sentimentality, poetic subjects, "poetic
thoughts," "poetic language," bombast, the moral standard of criticism, and divine inspiration. Throughout the last two-thirds of the
century Poe and Whitman successively were hewing away at these
poses. But each in his way was a lonely prophet rather than a pre-
cursor of the new poetry, which presently honored each of them
for some purposes but denied him for others. The consistent revolt
began in the '90's when young Robinson and Frost, without
knowledge of each other, started experimenting with the then revo-
lutionary notions which have remained the foundations of all our
modern poetry, namely honest individual emotion, the availability
of any experience as material for poetry, the language of common
speech, the aesthetic standard of criticism, the sources of creativity
in imagination and hard work instead of in divinity.

In a large sense, what Robinson and Frost were doing was to take
positions of leadership in the aesthetic aspect of the gathering re-
pudiation of the whole standardized, emotionally artificial fabric of
late nineteenth-century American culture. By the end of the first
decade of the twentieth century the revolt was in full swing on
every religious, social, and intellectual front. Lindsay, Masters,
Harriet Monroe, Amy Lowell, the early Pound, and many others

helped integrate the prominent poetic subdivision of it in the "Renaissance of 1912," with its codification of Robinson's and Frost's ideas into what are still the three organic doctrines of modern poetry, professed by all four of the movements that have been mentioned, namely Reality of Experience, Reality of Expression, and Conscious Artistry. The poets, with their retinue of critics and increasingly converted public, were "unacknowledged legislators" in a wonderfully swift and thorough revolution. Between 1910 and 1920 every significant feature of the very highly perfected social and intellectual system of the eighties and nineties was expressly denied, deliberately violated, and removed from the textbook of youth.

Thus the Lost Generation, the generation following Robinson and Frost and comprising their younger contemporaries, found themselves straddling a gulf. Having been born in the '90's and so raised in the old elaborate culture, they assisted in its destruction in their youth, mostly before the First War, and faced maturity without any integrating god, philosophy, social conviction, or ethic. Their only concrete affirmation was of the doctrine of self-expression, divided into the related channels of sexual expression, as conveniently adapted from Freud, and aesthetic expression typified by the manifestos of 1912, with considerable academic influence from Croce. As for any beliefs that might give central meaning to both individual and social life, the Lost Generation stood precariously over a void where not even the wreckage of their native Victorianism remained. The effort to fill the abyss with a new spiritual, intellectual and social structure, a new culture, began immediately with their intellectuals and it continues today. Some advance toward a humanist ethic has been made. But no comprehensive interpretation of life or of the puzzle of Being has gathered momentum. On the contrary, the general trend of successive youth, accelerated by the disillusionments of the thirties and the Second War, has for fifty years been less upward towards any new affirmation than downward into positivist common sense, relativism, pluralism, and negation that varies from gentle agnosticism to aggressive cynicism and nihilism.

In this descending procession the romantic poets of the twenties hold a paradoxical position. As leaders of the great demolition, they were more deliberately and actually destructive than any leadership or any generation that has followed them; but at the same time they were more affirmative instinctively. They had been bred in a time when almost everybody still suspected that there was some Meaning of life and the cosmos—usually called God. However honest their rational iconoclasm might be, they were supplied by inheritance and early environment with an instinct for abstract truth and with imagination that was under compulsion to make it concrete. Wherefore, however profound the disillusionment out of which they spoke, their poetry made absolute demands upon the human and cosmic continuum, and it made them with the power of compressed frustration. Wherefore, whether or not they arrived at any truth, and whether any truth they arrived at involved absolute negation or absolute affirmation, their poetic output contains more work with the sweep of greatness than does the combined output of the rest of American poetic history.

The bulk of the poetry of the twenties was romantic because it epitomized at least three of the four recognized qualities that distinguish romanticism from classicism. *First*, in its instinctive quest for absolute truth to replace the old God lost, it exhibited that *Motility* which is in contrast with the *Static* quality of classic poetry. The romantic is always going somewhere. He is bound for a country in whose reality he believes though he has not seen it; he affirms truth that he has not yet grasped. The classicist, on the other hand, knows where he lives, he knows the limits of his house, and of his country, of his percepts and his concepts. And he accepts them. He takes his stand in truth already surveyed and recorded. The romantic searches for "far off things," whether backward toward "battles long ago," or outward into fantasies of "magic casements" and "perilous seas," or forward "beyond the sunset." He is a potential mystic, in search of transcendent truth. To be sure, he may stop on the way at some systematic humanism or religious orthodoxy, and so be reborn a classicist. Likewise, if he arrives at mystical reality he is thenceforth a settled mystic and no longer a travelling romantic. Yet in both cases his habit of motility is likely to persist in his writing and to keep him in the category of romantic poets. Incidentally, it is not intended to imply here that a classicist may not also be a mystic. Unlike the romantic, his search for truth will be rational and methodical; but that does not forestall his arriving at revelation by a leap of imaginative perception exactly as the romantic may. As has been the case with many Christian mystics, one can at once believe in a reasoned system and enjoy mystical perception of the center of it. In fact, as will be suggested presently, some such combination of reason and imagination may characterize the new culture toward which we are tending.

The *Second* common aspect of romanticism that distinguished most of the poets of the twenties was their *Subjectivity* in contrast to the *Objectivity* of classicism. They were concerned with themselves and where they were going, and external objects were primarily important only as bearing on their quest. This distinction, while sound, must be qualified by the reminder that where the original subjective emotion moves out into an object, as it usually does, it penetrates it more intimately than does the classical, originally objective impulse, the latter being content to describe in detail the surface of the object, together with its significant, external relations. The standard contrast is between Gray's classical *Elegy*, with its smooth surface and large general statement, and Crabbe's romantic *The Village*—published only thirty years later—which expresses the poet's personal identification with the rural poor and actually portrays them to the reader's imagination.

The *Third* recognized mark of romanticism that qualified most of the poetry of the twenties was the natural concomitant of the motility and the subjectivity. This was subconscious—or unconscious—*Emotion* as distinguished from the conscious and demonstrative *Reason* that characterizes classical work. The conscious artifice of the surface of the poem was thin enough to let through more of the light of the original, unconscious, imaginative perception than comes through the generally more finished craftsmanship of classical poetry. In making this and the other common distinctions it is, of course, always necessary to remember that they are matters of degree. Supposedly "cold" reason is a rudimentary form of "hot" imagination. Each is a magic leap of the mind, confronted with data, to a resolution, called a conclusion in the case of reason, and a perception in the case of imagination. The difference in "heat" is a function of a difference in direction of the leap. In a classical poem, the leap of reason is outward, not only to perfect the surface of the poem, but to synthesize consciously the object observed with other objects or cases and to integrate them into a concept, principle or law. In a romantic poem, the leap of imagination is inward to perceive subconsciously a new and essential quality of the object, whether it be the self, an image, a cosmos, or an idea. In both leaps there is pleasure. But in the romantic poem it is more concentrated and ecstatic. In the classical poem it is more stately, cooler, more widely diffused in universal application. Verticality and horizontality. Chartres against the Parthenon.

A *Fourth* distinction between romantic and classical poetry involves the charge that romantic poetry is *Obscure* where classic poetry is *Clear*. As between the neo-romanticism of the twenties or the standard romanticism of the early nineteenth century, and the true classicism of Milton, Dryden and Pope, this charge is just. For clarity in the prose sense is a primary aim of truly classical verse.

The application of the above four criteria to the poetry of the New Criticism, which was the chief rival of neo-romanticism in the twenties and the thirties, shows why I call it "semi" classical. It meets two of the four requirements of classicism, namely static rather than motile content, and objective rather than subjective motivation. But of the other two criteria it violates one by excess and repudiates the other entirely. Seizing the general modern doctrine of self-conscious or rational artistry, the semi-classicals, starting with *The Waste Land* and ending with Pound's *Cantos*, carried it to the degree of denying and suppressing the intuitive or unconscious motive in poetic composition, the element of imagination which Dryden, Pope and Johnson admitted as indispensable, in a moderate or classical degree, to "what oft was thought but ne'er so well expressed." Furthermore, in their snobbish search for esoteric images, symbols and language which would be beyond the understanding of the herd, they reversed the fourth traditional distinction between classicism and romanticism, producing compilations of obscurity before which the most intricate tropes of Shelley or Robinson—which they professed to find difficult—are of a translucent clarity. Because of their suppression of imagination, the New Critics and the semi-classical poets—often the same individuals—will be remembered chiefly for their prose, and for no poem that has come to my attention except Eliot's later ones. Their failure in this respect is in contrast to the performance of the truly classical poets who, though a small minority in the twenties, contributed a disproportionate amount to the great poetry of the period and so to this collection.

The differences between romanticism and classicism are sufficient to have motivated many battles of many books. And they will continue to do so because both impulses are essential in literature as they are in the human adventure generally, and neither has meaning but by reference to the other. Romanticism is the aspiration toward the solution of the central Puzzle that is for many the strongest compulsion of the mind. And classicism is the pattern of the solution, the truth, or the perfection, which romanticism is seeking. Romanticism is mysticism on the move but not yet realized. Classicism is the pattern of the realization sought. Romanticism, unperverted into fancy, sentimentality or rhetoric, is the unique distinction and power of mankind. It is what does not surrender. Classicism is the fastness it may finally capture and accept. The demands of both romanticism and classicism are at all times active in healthy minds. The young romantic bears his classical adulthood in his dream of perfection. The soul of the classicist is the romantic he once was. Instead of a single ascent into enclosed peace, there is, for poets while they are poets, an alternation of climb and consolidation, climb and consolidation. Wordsworth and Emerson reached repose in their respective pantheisms, but they continued to explore.

Both kinds of poetry involve the same basic elements, and their differences are in degree. There is no great classical poem without traces of passionate, imaginative perception, like the experiences of "partial" Grace; there is no excellent romantic poem whose surface isn't consciously polished into appropriate rhetoric. Between the two categories there is enough difference in the thickness of the rational, conscious surface to justify the technical distinction. But it is important to remember that each type of poetry at its best contains some of the other's prerogative. Classicists and romanticists agree on the definition of poetry as the unliteral or tropeic use of language to stimulate the imagination of the reader to a recognition of the poet's original, subconscious perception. And they agree that the language in the finished poem must have suffered long under the pruning knife and file. They agree upon the ingredients, and they understand each other. They disagree only in the proportions in the prescription.

In application of the above distinction, my appraisal is that of the thirty-three poets included in this book, four are almost purely classical; three are dominantly classical but with romantic features; eleven are romantic but with some classical features; and fifteen are almost purely romantic. If my selection of thirty-three poets with one or more "great" poems each is a fair sampling of the professional poetic population of a little under three hundred in the twenties, then the implication is that about three-quarters of that population were of a dominantly romantic disposition.

My assemblage in this book of one hundred poems or excerpts all but three of which I call "great" requires a careful definition of that banal epithet. Of all the vague terms in the vocabulary of English criticism, it is surely the vaguest, being commonly used as a loose synonym for "excellent," or merely "good." I use the word in its literal sense, as signifying a quantitative rather than a qualitative standard. In the poet it defines a perception which involves a "great" amout of his potential imaginative perception. The reader's cortex, supposedly infinite in capacity, is a screen upon which all of his experience has been imprinted and which, thus adorned, hangs in the subconscious darkness of every day. Minor poetry is a flashlight which projects the reader's imagination in a single beam to light with extreme clarity, or poetic "purity," a small area of the screen, a small bundle of images, or a simple concept or two. Great poetry is a stereopticon lantern from which the imagination spreads to illumine, sometimes crudely, a large part of the screen, perhaps all of it, perhaps a potential panorama larger than the particular reader's experience so that the content of the poem is only partially perceived. The joy of imaginative illumination is commensurately great; it is overwhelming, like the receipt of Grace in which everything is plain and the self is dissolved.

It seems to me important to insist on the use of the word "great" in this its literal, quantitative sense, chiefly in order to distinguish great poetry from minor poetry which is usually "better," "purer," more "excellent" than most great poetry is. It is possible to find short poems that are both great and excellent. But it would be difficult to find over a page of great poetry that was not somewhere flat with versified prose or rough with rhetoric for its own sake—rhetoric the showy pretender who is always waiting to shoulder in and substitute for great poetry. For inclusion here, a poem or passage must have an imaginative or poetic aura, either in overtone or in pervasive tropeic expression in detail. It must be poetry. But in two or three cases where the panorama of perception is very large, I have been commensurately less exacting in the requirement of poetic saturation. After all, a great perception is itself an act of imagination, and so throws some poetic aura even over a text that is otherwise literal and prosaic.

The distinction between greatness and excellence is evident on the immortal shelf. Great poetry is immortal because of the inclusiveness of its content which will remain so for all mankind, future as well as present. Minor poetry, when it is immortal, has for its only credential its excellence as poetry, its exquisite perfection in both tropeic uses and verbal music. One could make a very small list of the most distinguished, but not the greatest, poets in literature who survive for their excellence alone. It would include Sappho, Catullus, Heine, Herrick, Marvell, Coleridge, Keats, Housman, H.D., Hillyer and Frost. The list of the world's greatest poets, not counting the dramatists, would also be small. It would include Homer, Vergil, Lucretius, Dante, Goethe, Hugo, Chaucer, Milton, Wordsworth and Robinson. These poets have written not only a few great poems but a large body of great poetry, much of it in long poems which are rarely read. Besides Robinson, other candidates from America would be Whitman and, from the twenties, Eliot, Stevens and Jeffers. As for the other poets in these contents, each of them, in my opinion, wrote one or more great poems but not enough to qualify him for the small list of the world's greatest.

The distinction between Frost and Robinson is specially illustrative of the two categories presented here. Frost was a much "better" poet. It would be hard to improve a line or a phrase of his. Also he wrote three or four poems of the caliber of greatness. Robinson, on the other hand, wrote a great deal of versified prose, and occasional bursts of prosaic rhetoric. Yet the psychic world he inhabited, as revealed by the bulk of his work and scores of single poems, comprised all of mankind in general and most of it in particular, whereas Frost, with few exceptions, confined his perceptions and his reports of them to his and his neighbors' farms whose prospects were less than cosmic and whose populations were less than universal. Wherefore, Frost comes off with the honor of being chief among the distinguished minor poets of America, and Robinson with the honor of being the least in the temple of the great poets of the world. For insisting on this substantial and quantitative standard of greatness, I shall doubtless be accused of trying to restore the nineteenth-century moral standard of criticism, or at least some kind of extra-aesthetic standard. To which my comment is that the fallacy of the moral standard was not so much in its being extra-aesthetic as in its being false, a figment of the hypocritical moralism of a dying culture. The standard of greatness, of the greatest possible engagement of imagination, is a standard of truth at any time, irrespective of specific morals or general culture. If the formal and substantial perceptions of the imagination be admitted as psychologically identical, it must follow that they are also identically subject to the standard of beauty.

The question of the inclusion in this collection of three hybrid Anglo-American poets I have solved by arbitrary hair-splitting. Eliot, although residentially an Englishman during the twenties, and eventually a British subject, yet was both American-born and influential upon America's poetic consciousness throughout the twenties and thirties: wherefore, he is included. Sylvia Townsend Warner has always been an Englishwoman; yet she is included because she lived in America through much of the twenties and was actively part of the American literary world as a critic, a novelist and a poet. Auden, on the other hand, though he lived here through the forties and fifties and became eventually an American citizen, yet is excluded because he did not come to this country until 1939 and, although he was known, was of little influence before that.

The selection presented here is not limited to poems actually written, or even published, in the twenties, rather to the work of poets whose central period of production at least overlapped that decade. The one exception is Santayana, whose sonnets were published in 1906; I include three of them here because their attitude of romantic groping out of despair was characteristic of the Lost Generation and prescient of the twenties, because his sonnets generally were popular with the poets then, and because he was active in other publishing in that decade. After Santayana, Masters and Robinson are the oldest poets included here. Masters's best work was published between 1915 and '20, though he issued more volumes in the twenties. Robinson's *Luke Havergal* was first privately printed in 1896, but it was hardly read until the appearance of his first *Collected Poems* in 1922; Robinson's period of greatest production was between 1917 (*Merlin*) and 1931 (*Matthias at the Door*), and his three Pulitzer Prizes were all in the twenties. Frost's publication stretched between 1913 and the forties, and his Pulitzer Prizes were in 1923, 1930 and 1935. Of publication later than the twenties, Eliot's *Four Quartets* did not appear in America until the early forties, but his high influence began in 1922. In three cases I have included less than great but near great poems, two because, like Santayana's sonnets, they were peculiarly typical of the twenties, and one to bolster up an otherwise weak section. In pursuance of emphasizing greatness over excellence, I have included three poets whose large panoramas are often defaced by rhetorical or dramatic, versified prose; the elimination of these blemishes accounted for much of the cutting and excerpting. Finally, I have exercised what seems to have become the anthologist's fatuous prerogative; I have included four pieces of my own.

Chiefly with the object of rescuing some great passages from a matrix of over-writing, I have frequently committed the supposed sacrilege of excerpting. Under the New Critics' emphasis upon esoteric excellence, long poems, which rarely meet that standard as whole units, have passed into disrepute. And in consequence much of the greatest poetry of the twenties, thirties and forties lies languishing, sandwiched between slabs of mediocre writing—like much of the same in Shakespeare, Milton and Wordsworth. I know of no way of trying to reverse this drift of many major passages toward oblivion except to lift them out of their padding and make them stand alone. I am attempting this method, although it involves two serious difficulties. First, it thins some passages by removing their frame of preliminary exposition and terminal, dramatic resolution. And sometimes it was blocked by the refusal of controllers of copyright to permit excerpting. Nevertheless, I submit that this is a practice which should be followed, in order to preserve the best poetry in the language. And, incidentally, it should have a material appeal to both poets and publishers in encouraging the sales both of separately published long poems and of collected volumes.

The topical arrangement of the ten sections into which the book is divided follows a loose dramatic progression. The first section announces the dominant theme of the twenties, namely "Romantic Affirmation," the assertion by the Lost Generation that some yet undiscovered truth existed, while also finding reality in the romantic search for its own sake. The second, third and fourth sections state the fashionable formulas for truth that the poets of the twenties expected to find, namely the general rule of Self-expression and its two chief applications Sex and Beauty. The next five sections deal with less special aspects of experience, the eighth presenting the poets' summary comments on life, together with the solutions, short of mystical revelation, that some of them reached. The final section presents the "Mystical Realization" of those few who attained and proclaimed it, the confirmation of the original Romantic Affirmation.

Among the ten sections of the book there is much possible overlapping. Many poems in the more general sections, those dealing with "Self," "The Human Condition," "Death," and "Mystical Realization," might equally belong in the more special ones. I have favored the general sections in order to emphasize the more inclusive, which is to say the "greater," features of the poems. Although there was a little socio-political comment in the poetry of the twenties, it was the principal feature of that of the thirties; wherefore, in order to emphasize the distinction between the decades, there is here no separate section with that title, and what socio-political writing there was of large caliber is in the section on "The Human Condition." Metaphysical speculation, also atypical of the twenties, is divided between the sections on "The Human Condition" and "Mystical Realization."

But for the comparison of Robinson and Frost, introduced to clarify the principal distinction between greatness and excellence which is assumed everywhere in the text, criticism of particular poets will be found in the headnotes of the sections. Where a poet appears in more than one section, comment on him is usually divided. In any array of thirty-three poets, it does not seem unreasonable to ask the reader, desiring to note all the comment on a particular one, to follow him through the brief table of contents. Because of the same limited inclusion of poets and poems, there is no index.

I must confess that in selecting the contents I have attended carefully only to the sixty-five or so poets of the twenties who received respectable publication and favorable comment. This lazy method has surely resulted in the omission of several great poems which the injustices of personal idiosyncracy or critical fashion and snobbery denied a hearing. I would be grateful for reminders of any of these in order that I may attempt restitution where it seems to be due.

In spite of the mistakes of exclusion and inclusion that have probably been made, I dare hope that the contents supports the introductory assertions: that the twenties, loosely delimited, was the period of the largest outburst of poetry this country has known; that it was dominantly a romantic outburst; and that many of the young poets today, disillusionized alike with rationalistic semi-classicism and ego-centric colloquialism, are looking back at its output with interest. This is neither to prophesy a romantic revival nor to deny the possibility of a genuinely classical one, for both are among the possibilities. The future is doubtless forming in divers spiritual and social trends which few if any prophets are yet able to see coalescing in integrated cultural rebirth. The obvious signs are negative and ominous for all poetry. Already we are in the age of specialization in which each art, including poetry, tends to become, like each science, an exclusive club exercising in its own language for the edification of its own initiates. Already we are in the technological age in which the human imagination that is impelled to deal with unmeasurable things may be bred out of the genes, and *homo sapiens* devolve into an infinitely rational new form of *homo erectus*, the fellow who lived and roamed before the imagination with its gods, spirits and practical as well as impractical visions, ousted him from the caves and exterminated him. In the technological age also, the imagination that looks for inner realities, instead of being bred out, may be seduced and perverted to material hypothecation by the apparently limitless possibilities of speculation and exploration in the fields of both macroscopic and microscopic space. Under the social domination of this specialization and this technology it would seem likely that any prosodic practices that survive will be recondite, rational and superclassical.

And yet, at a time when all of these signs are obvious around us, there are counter-signs in the fact just referred to, namely that a respectable proportion of young poets today, and of college students generally, are expressing boredom at the prospect of a life circumscribed by the analytical rationalism that destroyed the religions of their great-grandfathers, dichotomized their grandfathers, and led their fathers into aesthetic and humanistic postures that have no relation to the Eternal Puzzle. It may well be that in the midst of the welter of experimental materialism a new search for immaterial truth is already rising and that this new school of proto-romantic poets is the rolling foam on the wave.

If there is a paradox between these classical and romantic tendencies, it may well be the literary aspect of an equally paradoxical trend in the age, the trend that would reconcile the ancient and always absurd controversy between science and religion. Surely all affirmative modern philosophers, from Christian Existentialists through Russell and Whitehead, have been working toward this reconciliation, this unification of the two great and related human functions of reason and imagination. Surely all affirmative contemporary theologians, from Tillich through Bonhoeffer, Bultmann, the others mentioned in Bishop Robinson's *Honest to God*, and above all Teilhard de Chardin, are working toward a new Christian symbolism which will retain unaltered the fundamental, transcendental truths, while implementing them in a new mythology acceptable to science, a mythology, for example, based in the latest timetables of paleontology or the last developments of Jungian psychology.

If such a reunion of materialism and immaterialism, of analysis and intuition, is to be the focal point of the new culture that we have been awaiting since 1900, it is not difficult to prognosticate that the poetic aspect of it will be a comparable reconciliation between traditional classicism and traditional romanticism. The classical emphasis upon conscious art, which after all has been in our poetic bloodstream since the 1890's, will be reaffirmed, and indeed may well tend into some new formalism replacing the traditional formalism which both the Imagists of the early twenties and the recent anarchistic Colloquials proscribed. But the new rationalism will not be carried to the point of denial of the subconscious imagination in substantial creativeness, in the fashion of the recent semi-classicists, or even to the point of clothing the imagination and its perceptions in an armor of formal elegance, as was the practice of the true classicists of the late seventeenth and eighteenth centuries. Rather, in the poetic aspect of the new culture the unconscious imagination will be recognized and invited by the conscious reason, for both technical and substantial purposes. The result may well be a poetry in which the old distinctions are forgotten, a poetry combining the conscious, classical excellence of Milton or Pope with the unconscious, romantic, imaginative sweep of Wordsworth, Shelley, Robinson, Jeffers, or the Eliot of the *Four Quartets*. At last imagination will acknowledge the necessary contribution of reason to the sense of beauty or form. And at last reason will recognize that the ultimate mystery is as far as ever beyond the ken of the telescope and microscope, that only the imagination can perceive it and only great poetry can name it.

Chard Powers Smith

❀ ROMANTIC AFFIRMATION

✿ *Romantic Affirmation, the assertion of truth not yet reached,* or simply of the reality of the journey for its own sake, is of course not peculiar to the 1920's. Its aspiration has characterized all the romantic periods, from that of Chaucer, through those of Shakespeare and Wordsworth. But in contrast to the lorn escapism of the decadent romanticism of the end of the nineteenth century, and to the esoteric rationality of the semi-classical school that became dominant in America in the late thirties, romantic affirmation is indeed a distinguishing feature of the poetry of the forty years between. But for the seven or eight dominantly classical poems included in this volume, its abstract impulsion, whether of what I shall presently call the teleological or what I shall call the marching sort, characterizes the rest.

The two lyrics that open the section, *Luke Havergal* and *Stopping by Woods on a Snowy Evening*, are alike in romantic motility, in classical precision of expression, and in a haunting, monotonous music that helps the respective universal overtones. Because of these likenesses, their differences are the more striking. They illustrate well the contrasts between their two poets. Both were New England mystics, Frost of the elementary, pantheistic sort, Robinson combining that with metaphysical, self-losing Christianity. Both were at the source of the doctrines of honest experience, honest expression and conscious art which are the foundation of modern American poetry, and together they were generally recognized in the twenties as the two leading poets of the day. In *Luke Havergal*, the personal emotion of the subject—or of the poet—though transmuted into an imaginative percept, yet glows through the art. In order to come to his mystical resolution beyond the "western gate," Luke must go through self-renunciation and suffering. But in *Stopping by Woods* the personal emotion is gentled away in the snowstorm. There are still duties in the world—"promises to keep"—and a long road ahead—"miles to go before I sleep." But none of this provides much obstacle to the narrator's and the reader's easy elevation through the veil of snow into identification with impersonal and motile, ultimate Being. Although Robinson usually writes in either the third person or the first person plural, yet the passion of his subjects, or of himself, is almost always evident. Frost, on the other hand, usually writes in the first person, yet the passion of the poet, or of his characters, is almost entirely submerged in the objective perception. By the criterion of personal emotion portrayed, Robinson's poetry is on the romantic side, Frost's on the classical side.

Yet in ideational terms the case is opposite. *Luke Havergal,* and most of Robinson's people, are in search of peace, classical repose, at the end of the quest. But Frost, while often, as here, on the verge of settled, mystical realization, yet is already on the move again as he almost comes to rest. All Being is in the quiet snowstorm in the woodlot; but the nature of Being is not in repose but in continuing motion for its own sake, "the sweep of easy wind and downy flake," or in *The Sound of Trees* in Frost's other poem in this section. At heart he was a motile romantic, in art an impersonal classicist. At heart Robinson was a settled classicist, in art a personal romantic. If we wish, we may recognize in them two different attitudes of romantics in their quests for mystical realization. Robinson usually represented the Teleological attitude which, while in motion, yet affirms an end, in or out of time, that will at length be attained, the school whose traditional pattern poem might be taken to be Wordsworth's *Tintern Abbey.* Frost's was the Travelling attitude that finds reality in the quest for its own sake and looks for no grail, the attitude whose great pattern poem is Tennyson's *Ulysses.* The distinction is far from universal, and most romantic poets provide examples of both kinds of affirmation. Robinson's *Miniver Cheevy* is an obvious case of yearning for its own sake, and Frost's two poems in the final section of this book are both statements of achieved realization. Many of Shelley's poems bespeak both attitudes, and the sweet sadness of Wordsworth's "unhappy far-off things" is near the origin of the travelling tradition. It was this sweet sadness, this pining "for what is not," that led nineteenth-century romanticism, largely by way of Tennyson and Longfellow, into the perversion that is the perennial threat to romanticism, namely sentimentality, the enjoyment of emotion for its own sake. This was the central object of the revolt of modern American poetry which Robinson and Frost led.

I greatly regret that it is not permitted to present excerpts from

Eliot's *Four Quartets*. In an anthology of this size there is not room to quote more than one of them entire; but even with space I would not quote them all, for they are irregular both in poetic excellence and in greatness. In this section I should like to have quoted the more inclusive passages of *East Coker* with their marching romantic aspiration—"In my end is my beginning." Once Eliot was past his satirical phase, epitomized in *The Waste Land*, in which incidentally he and Pound provided the waiting Americans with semi-classical obscurantism, he moved slowly into both romanticism and greatness. *Ash Wednesday* is still blurred as poetry by recondite, scholarly uses, but in its declaration of humility as an end, with a hint of light beyond, it intimates a hesitant affirmation. In the *Four Quartets* Eliot largely abandons his esoteric habits and New Critical following as his affirmation of mystical "hints and guesses" becomes progressively positive. In *East Coker* he reaches only as far as the travelling attitude, the necessity of eternal mobility, unending progress through deeper communion to deeper communion, the strong aspiration of *Ulysses*—duly plagiarized for imagery. In *The Dry Salvages*, which is the most consistent of the four both for excellence and for greatness, and which I shall quote entire in the last section of the book, he arrives at mystical certainty in so far as it is in him to do so.

The imagery of Crane's *Proem: To Brooklyn Bridge*, at once soaring and anchored, is a symbol of the uncompromising affirmation, the teleological type of romanticism, of the whole great poem it introduces and of the whole life of its potentially great poet who must choose death when he despaired of any absolute in the modern world. The second passage quoted, from the "Cape Hatteras" section of the poem, emphasizes the near identity of his quest with Whitman's democratic one, with Whitman's ultimate peace of the sea along Paumonok which Crane thought to find somewhere between Mexico and New York, having failed to find it in either. Dying in 1932, at the age of thirty-three, Crane was transitional between the romanticism of the twenties and the semi-classicism which eventually displaced it. He was transitional because, although romantic faith was his dominant quality, he was enough affected by the *avant garde* movement that later became the New

Criticism, to feel the necessity of straining for originality in figuration. Thus he sometimes slows the reader to conscious inquiry into what ought to be taken with unconscious speed.

Marianne Moore went along with the *avant garde* until, in the forties, she was the darling of the New Critics because of her exotic, encyclopedic allusions, especially in the fields of zoology and botany. And yet the impulse behind her fancy images seems quite different from the snobbish one of *The Waste Land*, of the later Pound, and of some of the lesser New Critical poets, who proposed to overwhelm the bourgeois reader with learning and so dispense with him. One feels that Miss Moore's colorful beasts and plants are paraded simply because she finds them fun, because she hopes the reader will enjoy them as much as she does, which the reader duly does. No matter how obscure the allusions in her tropes, they seem almost always to perform their poetic job of transmitting an imaginative perception, and the reader feels no impulse to turn to the dictionary and so lose the thread of the progress of imagination.

In this playful vein, for which Miss Moore is perhaps best known, she is not only a classical poet but a minor classical poet who surely would not want to qualify under my weighty and vulgar standard of greatness. But there is another Miss Moore who does meet my standard in a ponderous fashion that may embarrass the gay poet of the tricorn hat and the sequins. She has a dozen or more poems, some of them longish, which not only express a nobility of perception—which accounts for their inclusion here—but tend to do it in a flat style which all of her fancy line-setting can not elevate out of solid, powerful, rhetorical prose. Not only that, but some of these poems have a touch of romanticism, and the one of them that seems to me the all-round best, being the shortest and rising into great poetry at the end, is not only romantic but belongs to the marching school which affirms only the aspiration itself and looks to no end. Miss Moore's *What Are Years?* is not quite typical of this school because the reality of action for her is not in the marching "on the open road" toward an unknown end beyond the sunset, but it is in being trapped, straining to reach truth through the bars, and exulting in the effort. It is the marching prescription for life, effort for its own sake, but the kind of effort, as in everything else about Miss Moore, is original.

Frost's *The Sound of Trees*, closing this section, returns us from Miss Moore's eloquent prose to almost pure poetry. Like *What Are Years?* its greatness is in its end which summarizes romantic aspiration in all its aspects.

Luke Havergal

EDWIN ARLINGTON ROBINSON

Go to the western gate, Luke Havergal,
There where the vines cling crimson on the wall,
And in the twilight wait for what will come.
The leaves will whisper there of her, and some,
Like flying words, will strike you as they fall;
But go, and if you listen she will call.
Go to the western gate, Luke Havergal—
Luke Havergal.

No, there is not a dawn in eastern skies
To rift the fiery night that's in your eyes;
But there, where western glooms are gathering,
The dark will end the dark, if anything:
God slays Himself with every leaf that flies,
And hell is more than half of paradise.
No, there is not a dawn in eastern skies—
In eastern skies.

Out of a grave I come to tell you this,
Out of a grave I come to quench the kiss
That flames upon your forehead with a glow
That blinds you to the way that you must go.
Yes, there is yet one way to where she is,
Bitter, but one that faith may never miss.
Out of a grave I come to tell you this—
To tell you this.

There is the western gate, Luke Havergal,
There are the crimson leaves upon the wall.
Go, for the winds are tearing them away,—
Nor think to riddle the dead words they say,
Nor any more to feel them as they fall;
But go, and if you trust her she will call.
There is the western gate, Luke Havergal—
Luke Havergal.

Stopping by Woods on a Snowy Evening

ROBERT FROST

Whose woods these are I think I know.
His house is in the village though;
He will not see me stopping here
To watch his woods fill up with snow.

My little horse must think it queer
To stop without a farmhouse near
Between the woods and frozen lake
The darkest evening of the year.

He gives his harness bells a shake
To ask if there is some mistake.
The only other sound's the sweep
Of easy wind and downy flake.

The woods are lovely, dark and deep.
But I have promises to keep,
And miles to go before I sleep,
And miles to go before I sleep.

[from *The Bridge*]

Lines from *Proem: To Brooklyn Bridge*

HART CRANE

How many dawns, chill from his rippling rest
The seagull's wings shall dip and pivot him,
Shedding white rings of tumult, building high
Over the chained bay waters Liberty—

.   .   .

And Thee, across the harbor, silver-paced
As though the sun took step of thee, yet left
Some motion ever unspent in thy stride,—
Implicitly thy freedom staying thee!

.   .   .

Again the traffic lights that skim thy swift
Unfractioned idiom, immaculate sigh of stars,
Beading thy path—condense eternity:
And we have seen night lifted in thine arms.

Under thy shadow by the piers I waited;
Only in darkness is thy shadow clear.
The City's fiery parcels all undone,
Already snow submerges an iron year   .   .   .

O Sleepless as the river under thee,
Vaulting the sea, the prairies' dreaming sod,
Unto us lowliest sometime sweep, descend
And of the curveship lend a myth to God.

[from *The Bridge*]

Lines from *Cape Hatteras*

HART CRANE

And now, as launched in abysmal cupolas of space,
Toward endless terminals, Easters of speeding light—
Vast engines outward veering with seraphic grace
On clarion cylinders pass out of sight
To course that span of consciousness thou'st named
The Open Road—thy vision is reclaimed!
What heritage thou'st signalled to our hands!

And see! the rainbow's arch—how shimmeringly stands
Above the Cape's ghoul-mound, O joyous seer!
Recorders ages hence, yes, they shall hear
In their own veins uncancelled thy sure tread
And read thee by the aureole 'round thy head
Of pasture—shine, *Panis Angelicus!*

Afoot again, and onward without halt,—yes, Walt,
Not soon, nor suddenly,—No, never to let go
    My hand
            in yours,
                Walt Whitman—
                        so—

What Are Years?

MARIANNE MOORE

    What is our innocence,
what is our guilt? All are
    naked, none is safe. And whence
is courage: the unanswered question,

the resolute doubt,—
dumbly calling, deafly listening—that
in misfortune, even death,
    encourages others
    and in its defeat, stirs

   the soul to be strong? He
sees deep and is glad, who
   accedes to mortality
and in his imprisonment rises
upon himself as
the sea in a chasm, struggling to be
free, and unable to be,
    in its surrendering
    finds its continuing.

   So he who strongly feels,
behaves. The very bird,
   grown taller as he sings, steels
his form straight up. Though he is captive,
his mighty singing
says, satisfaction is a lowly
thing, how pure a thing is joy.

     This is mortality,
     this is eternity.

The Sound of Trees

ROBERT FROST

I wonder about the trees.
Why do we wish to bear
Forever the noise of these
More than another noise

So close to our dwelling place?
We suffer them by the day
Till we lose all measure of pace,
And fixity in our joys,
And acquire a listening air.
They are that that talks of going
But never gets away;
And that talks no less for knowing,
As it grows wiser and older,
That now it means to stay.
My feet tug at the floor
And my head sways to my shoulder
Sometimes when I watch trees sway,
From the window or the door.
I shall set forth for somewhere,
I shall make the reckless choice
Some day when they are in voice
And tossing so as to scare
The white clouds over them on.
I shall have less to say,
But I shall be gone.

✿ SELF

❀ *In the '20's the dominant implementation of romantic affirma*-tion was in terms of the doctrine of self. The reality of society was denied, as was the reality of all mystery except that of the ego and the id; no ethic was admitted except the callow one of self-expression, the then current phrase for self-indulgence. In its purity, the concept of the self and its realization were almost as abstract as the parent romantic affirmation, and in application it usually followed one or both of the intercommunicating channels of Sex and Art. Yet the abstraction alone was real and potent, looking to some super-sexual, super-aesthetic, subjective consummation that was neither the mystical "emptying of the self," nor the transcendental but less than mystical identification of the self with all Being. The abstract concept of self produced poetry at least as powerful as that produced by either of these, or by either of its two popular, tangible implementations.

The aggressive idea of self, being a denial of the basic human impulse to love, and being therefore evil, tended to conjure up as its own accompaniment, as part of itself, a sense of guilt. And this sense of guilt contributed violence to the expression that produced it. The poetry of abstract self-assertion, therefore, as distinguished from that of pure and unperverted romantic affirmation, tended to be a poetry of violence. Commonly, this violence took the self-justifying form of contemptuous attacks on the conventions and restraints of society, and on the human species for its loss of natural vigor and daring within its self-imposed shackles. Such an attack is Williams's *The Trees*, and the violence of its preachment of self-assertion is the more impressive because Williams was essentially a classicist who told only what he saw and had no impulse to take wing into any kind of transcendental nonsense.

More frequently, the attack on convention remained in its negative phase, leaving the assertion of self-expressive naturalism to be inferred. Such a negative cry is Amy Lowell's *Patterns*, and it is perhaps worth observing that in this negative aspect of the doctrine of self of the '20's we have one of the roots of that American matriarchy which grew in strength through the '30's and '40's. The men, having destroyed the religious and moral codes of the '80's and '90's through their hypocrisy, did not assert the traditional masculine prerogative to supply replacements, to go up on the mountain and come down with the tables and declare, "Thus saith the Lord." The doctrine of self-expression had no social or metaphysical aspect, and in theory at least, was congenial to the female or personal outlook. Wherefore, the men joined the women in the female prerogative of rattling the chains of restraint, without having any program to advance after freedom should be won. This was the period when the intellectuals began reading Marx with sympathy, undisturbed by his lack of any political blueprint or even theory on which to build a permanent or self-perpetuating government after the bourgeois evils had been destroyed.

In *Whale* William Rose Benét makes fun of what was left of the men after the relinquishment of their ancient prerogatives, nothing but their stark masculine selves, their essential maleness, a bulk of bombastic pretense, of absurd and dependent pomposity. Unlike his brother Stephen, William Benét had a metaphysical sweep of imagination; but he also had an irrepressible sense of humor which threw a haze of lightness over his efforts at mystical poetry. *Whale*, with its theme of masculine grandiloquence in the universe, allows him to combine his humor with his transcendental instinct without impairing either.

Jeffers was handicapped neither by humor, by any failure of masculine self-assurance, nor by classical reticence except as applied aesthetically in his versification. In *Cawdor* he combines self-assertion with rhetorical violence in what is perhaps the most powerful example of either in English. Here, as in most of his work, Jeffers—himself the gentlest of men—identified self-realization with carnal violence, an aristocratic "beaked desire" breaking through its padded straight-jacket of mediocrity. In comparison with the final, orgastic lines, the great traditional romantic expressions—Wordsworth's "battles long ago," Keats's "magic casements," even Tennyson's sailing "beyond the sunset"—are whispers. Only Shelley's self-assertion in *The West Wind* suggests comparison, and that remotely.

Although Stevens's first volume appeared in '23, he was less typically a poet of the twenties, or even the thirties, than he was of the forties with the New Critics and their intellectuality. He was not interested in mystical perception, let alone in the romantic search for its own sake, but in sober inquiry and conclusion. After Jeffers's

violence Stevens's gentle affirmation of the majesty of the self alone
creating cosmic reality, provides a return to static peace.

The Trees

WILLIAM CARLOS WILLIAMS

The trees—being trees
thrash and scream
guffaw and curse—
wholly abandoned
damning the race of men—

Christ, the bastards
haven't even sense enough
to stay out in the rain—

Wha ha ha ha

Wheeeeee
Clacka tacka tacka
tacka tacka
Wha ha ha ha ha
ha ha ha

knocking knees, buds
bursting from each pore
even the trunk's self
putting out leafheads—

Loose desire!
we naked cry to you—
"Do what you please."

You cannot!

—ghosts
sapped of strength

wailing at the gate
heartbreak at the bridgehead—
desire
dead in the heart

haw haw haw haw
—and memory broken

wheeeeee

There were never satyrs
never maenads
never eagle-headed gods—
These were men
from whose hands sprung
love
bursting in the wood—

Trees their companions
—a cold wind winterlong
in the hollows of our flesh
icy with pleasure—

no part of us untouched

Patterns

AMY LOWELL

I walk down the garden paths,
And all the daffodils
Are blowing, and the bright blue squills.

I walk down the patterned garden-paths
In my stiff, brocaded gown.
With my powdered hair and jewelled fan,
I too am a rare
Pattern. As I wander down
The garden paths.

My dress is richly figured,
And the train
Makes a pink and silver stain
On the gravel, and the thrift
Of the borders.
Just a plate of current fashion,
Tripping by in high-heeled, ribboned shoes.
Not a softness anywhere about me,
Only whalebone and brocade.
And I sink on a seat in the shade
Of a lime tree. For my passion
Wars against the stiff brocade.
The daffodils and squills
Flutter in the breeze
As they please.
And I weep;
For the lime-tree is in blossom
And one small flower has dropped upon my bosom.

And the plashing of waterdrops
In the marble fountain
Comes down the garden-paths.
The dripping never stops.
Underneath my stiffened gown
Is the softness of a woman bathing in a marble basin,
A basin in the midst of hedges grown
So thick, she cannot see her lover hiding,
But she guesses he is near,
And the sliding of the water
Seems the stroking of a dear
Hand upon her.

What is Summer in a fine brocaded gown!
I should like to see it lying in a heap upon the ground.
All the pink and silver crumpled up on the ground.

I would be the pink and silver as I ran along the paths,
And he would stumble after,
Bewildered by my laughter.
I should see the sun flashing from his sword-hilt
    and the buckles on his shoes.
I would choose
To lead him in a maze along the patterned paths,
A bright and laughing maze for my heavy-booted lover.
Till he caught me in the shade,
And the buttons of his waistcoat bruised my body
    as he clasped me,
Aching, melting, unafraid.
With the shadows of the leaves and the sundrops,
And the plopping of the waterdrops,
All about us in the open afternoon—
I am very like to swoon
With the weight of this brocade,
For the sun sifts through the shade.

Underneath the fallen blossom
In my bosom,
Is a letter I have hid.
It was brought to me this morning by a rider from the Duke.
"Madam, we regret to inform you that Lord Hartwell
Died in action Thursday se'nnight."
As I read it in the white, morning sunlight,
The letters squirmed like snakes.
"Any answer, Madam," said my footman.
"No," I told him.
"See that the messenger takes some refreshment.
No, no answer."
And I walked into the garden,
Up and down the patterned paths,
In my stiff, correct brocade.

The blue and yellow flowers stood up proudly in the sun,
Each one.
I stood upright too,
Held rigid to the pattern
By the stiffness of my gown.
Up and down I walked,
Up and down.

In a month he would have been my husband.
In a month, here, underneath this lime,
We would have broke the pattern;
He for me, and I for him,
He as Colonel, I as Lady,
On this shady seat.
He had a whim
That sunlight carried blessing.
And I answered, "It shall be as you have said."
Now he is dead.

In Summer and in Winter I shall walk
Up and down
The patterned garden-paths
In my stiff, brocaded gown.
The squills and daffodils
Will give place to pillared roses, and to asters, and to snow.
I shall go
Up and down,
In my gown.
Gorgeously arrayed,
Boned and stayed.
And the softness of my body will be guarded from embrace
By each button, hook, and lace.
For the man who should loose me is dead,
Fighting with the Duke in Flanders,
In a pattern called a war.
Christ! What are patterns for?

Whale

WILLIAM ROSE BENÉT

Rain, with a silver flail;
  Sun, with a golden ball;
Ocean, wherein the whale
  Swims minnow-small;

I heard the whale rejoice
  And cynic sharks attend;
He cried with a purple voice,
  "The Lord is my Friend!"

" 'With flanged and battering tail,
  With huge and dark baleen,'
He said, 'Let there be Whale
  In the Cold and Green!'

"He gave me a water-spout,
  A side like a harbor wall;
The Lord from cloud looked out
  And planned it all.

"With glittering crown atilt
  He leaned on a glittering rail;
He said, 'Where Sky is spilt,
  Let there be Whale.'

"Tier upon tier of wings
  Blushed and blanched and bowed;
Phalanxed fiery things
  Cried in the cloud;

"Million-eyed was the mirk
  At the plan not understood;
But the Lord looked on his work
  And saw it was good.

"He gave me marvelous girth
　For the curve of back and breast,
And a tiny eye of mirth
　To hide His jest.

"He made me a floating hill,
　A plunging deep-sea mine.
This was the Lord's will;
　The Lord is Divine.

"I magnify his name
　In earthquake and eclipse,
In weltering molten flame
　And wrecks of ships,

"In waves that lick the moon;
　I, the plow of the sea!
I am the Lord's boon;
　The Lord made me!"

The sharks barked from beneath,
　As the great whale rollicked and roared,
"Yes, and our grinning teeth,
　Was it not the Lord?"

Then question pattered like hail
　From fishes large and small.
"The Lord is mighty," said Whale,
　"The Lord made all!

"His is a mammoth jest
　Life may never betray;
He has laid it up in his breast
　Till Judgment Day;

"But high when combers foam
　And tower their last of all,

My power shall haul you home
  Through Heaven wall.

"A trumpet then in the gates,
  To the ramps a thundering drum,
I shall lead you where He waits
  For His Whale to come.

"Where His cloudy seat is placed
  On high in an empty dome,
I shall trail the Ocean abased
  In chains of foam.

"Unwieldy, squattering dread;
  Where the blazing cohorts stand
At last I shall lift my head
  As it feels His hand.

"Then wings with a million eyes
  Before mine eyes shall quail;
'Look you, all Paradise,
  I was His Whale!' "

I heard the Whale rejoice,
  As he splayed the waves to a fan:
"And the Lord shall say with His Voice
  'Leviathan!'

"The Lord shall say with His Tongue,
  'Now let all Heaven give hail
To my Jest when I was young,
  To my very Whale.' "

Then the Whale careened in the Sea,
  He floundered with flailing tail,
Flourished and rollicked he,
  "Aha! Mine Empery!

For the Lord said, 'Let Whale be!'
   And there was Whale!"

Lines from *Cawdor*

ROBINSON JEFFERS

. . . . At the one shot
The great dark bird leaped at the roof of the cage
In silence and struck the wood; it fell, then suddenly
Looked small and soft, muffled in its folded wings.

The nerves of men after they die dream dimly
And dwindle into their peace; they are not very passionate,
And what they had was mostly spent while they lived.
They are sieves for leaking desire; they have many pleasures
And conversations; their dreams too are like that.
The unsocial birds are a greater race,
Cold-eyed, and their blood burns. What leaped up to death,
The extension of one storm-dark wing filling its world,
Was more than the soft garment that fell. Something had
      flown away. Oh cage-hoarded desire,
Like the blade of a breaking wave reaped by the wind, or
      flame rising from fire, or cloud-coiled lightning
Suddenly unfurled in the cave of heaven: I that am
      stationed, and cold at heart, incapable of burning,
My blood like standing sea-water lapped in a stone pool,
      my desire to the rock, how can I speak of you?
Mine will go down to the deep rock.

            This rose,
Possessing the air over its emptied prison,
The eager powers at its shoulders waving shadowless
Unwound the ever-widened spirals of flight
As a star light, it spins the night-stabbing threads
From its own strength and substance: so the aquiline desire

Burned itself into meteor freedom and spired
Higher still, and saw the mountain-dividing
Canyon of its captivity .   .   .   .
.   .   .   .   like an old crack in a wall,
Violet-shadowed and gold-lighted; the little stain
Spilt on the floor of the crack was the strong forest;
The grain of sand was the Rock .   .   .   .

.   .   .

This burned and soared. The shining ocean below lay on
    the shore
Like the great shield of the moon come down, rolling
    bright rim to rim with the earth. Against it the multiform
And many-canyoned coast-range hills were gathered into
    one carven mountain, one modulated
Eagle's cry made stone, stopping the strength of the sea.
    The beaked and winged effluence
Felt the air foam under its throat and saw
The mountain sun-cup Tassajara, where fawns
Dance in the steam of the hot fountains at dawn,
Smoothed out, and the high strained ridges beyond Cachagua,
Where the rivers are born and the last condor is dead,
Flatten, and a hundred miles toward morning the Sierras
Dawn with their peaks of snow, and dwindle and smooth down
On the globed earth.

        It saw from the height and desert space of
    unbreathable air
Where meteors make green fire and die, the ocean dropping
    westward to the girdle of the pearls of dawn
And the hinder edge of the night sliding toward Asia; it
    saw far under eastward the April-delighted
Continent; and time relaxing about it now, abstracted
    from being, it saw the eagles destroyed,
Mean generations of gulls and crows taking their world:
    turn for turn in the air, as on earth
The white faces drove out the brown. It saw the white
    decayed and the brown from Asia returning;

It saw men learn to outfly the hawk's brood and forget it
    again; it saw men cover the earth and again
Devour each other and hide in caverns, be scarce as
    wolves. It neither wondered nor cared, and it saw
Growth and decay alternate forever, and the tides
    returning.

It saw, according to the sight of its kind, the archetype
Body of life a beaked carnivorous desire
Self-upheld on storm-broad wings: but the eyes
Were spouts of blood; the eyes were gashed out; dark blood
Ran from the ruinous eye-pits to the hook of the beak
And rained on the waste spaces of empty heaven.
Yet the great Life continued; yet the great Life
Was beautiful, and she drank her defeat, and devoured
Her famine for food.

        There the eagle's phantom perceived
Its prison and its wound were not its peculiar wretchedness,
All that lives was maimed and bleeding, caged or in
    blindness,
Lopped at the ends with death and conception, and shrewd
Cautery of pain on the stumps to stifle the blood, but not
Refrains for all that; life was more than its functions
And accidents, more important than its pains and pleasures,
A torch to burn in with pride, a necessary
Ecstasy in the run of the cold substance,
And scape-goat of the greater world. (But as for me,
I have heard the summer dust crying to be born
As much as ever flesh cried to be quiet.)
Pouring itself on fulfilment the eagle's passion
Left life behind and flew at the sun, its father.
The great unreal talons took peace for prey
Exultantly, their death beyond death; stooped upward,
    and struck
Peace like a white fawn in a dell of fire.

[from *Notes Toward
A Supreme Fiction*]

Lines from *It Must Give Pleasure*

WALLACE STEVENS

viii
What am I to believe? If the angel in his cloud,
Serenely gazing at the violent abyss,
Plucks on his strings to pluck abysmal glory,

Leaps downward through evening's revelations, and
On his spredden wings, needs nothing but deep
    space,
Forgets the gold centre, the golden destiny,

Grows warm in the motionless motion of his flight,
Am I that imagine this angel less satisfied?
Are the wings his, the lapis-haunted air?

Is it he or is it I that experience this?
Is it I then that keep saying there is an hour
Filled with expressible bliss, in which I have

No need, am happy, forget need's golden hand,
Am satisfied without solacing majesty,
And if there is an hour there is a day,

There is a month, a year, there is a time
In which majesty is a mirror of the self:
I have not but I am and as I am, I am.

These external regions, what do we fill them with
Except reflections, the escapades of death,
Cinderella fulfilling herself beneath the roof?

❀ SEX

❁ *The sexual aspect of the self-expression of the '20's not only* proposed to divorce the sexual self from the restraints of convention: it went further and, following Freud, proposed to divorce it from love. Love was associated with the other pretenses of the '80's and '90's, when it had in fact been as deeply buried under sentimentality as the crusaders of the '20's proposed to bury it under sensuality. As far as the men were concerned, love and sentimentality were the same, and they were not slow to accept the implications of a field day for masculine promiscuity. The women, far gone in feminism but still impelled to hear God speaking through the man, tried to adjust to the new law of liberty, and fondly hoped that by progressing from lover to lover they were making themselves over in the masculine image.

The claim to greatness of the two sonnets of Millay's in this section is their representation of this whole decade of society in which the intellectual women made the attempt, at once tragic and absurd, virtually to unsex themselves. The gamut of Millay's love sonnets is very large, all the way from the early girlish naughtiness to the nobility of renunciation which will be presented later. Midway in the ascent is this assertion of her self against the slavery of love, a declaration of independence in which she spoke for the intellectual women of the twenties and for which she was greatly admired.

Sylvia Townsend Warner's seeming folk tale *Nelly Trim* elevates sex into a kind of social idealism. Jeffers's *The Maid's Thought* identifies sex with the glory of spring and rebirth in nature. About half the stanzas of Cummings's *Epithalamion* do the same thing with pagan magnificence; but as the rest of the poem wanders afield in mythology, and as permission to excerpt is denied, I have used instead two of his erotic, so-called "sonnets."

Another example of pagan treatment of sex in the '20's is that of the witch dance, the celebration of black magic, in Aiken's *The House of Dust*. Here violence compensates for the unnaturalness of sex without love. The passages excerpted from this lengthy ritual are themselves not much padded by Aiken's frequent fault of overwriting, of listing illustrations and analogies *around* a point instead of stating the one perfect trope. Essentially a great poet in sweep of imagination, and thoroughly emancipated from the sentimental affectations of Victorian verse, he yet remained a little behind in the aesthetic revolution that Robinson and Frost started, the movement for compactness, for the *mot juste*, for conveying the experience itself instead of "thoughts" about it. Right through the '20's and '30's, Aiken was still writing like a thoroughly emancipated poet of the '80's. There is much of his that deserves inclusion in this anthology for greatness of concept but is disqualified for unpoetic diffuseness of verse.

In *Roan Stallion*, Jeffers raises sex beyond a ritual of nature and beyond any kind of idealism to stark, impersonal, superhuman, cosmic power, truth beyond time in the moment of the creative orgasm of elemental force.

In *Tristram*, Robinson brings sex back, at least nominally, to love. But he still denies it the continuity of actual love by insisting repeatedly in great poetry that the lovers are outside of time, thus identifying love with the timeless or orgastic moment. When the timeless moment is denied them there is nothing else for them, no other form that love can take; there is only death. Robinson wrote *Tristram* in impatience at being called a "dry New England psychologist." He could not do less than ennoble sex beyond anything his contemporaries made of it. But the epic is slight in comparison with *Lancelot*, where the theme of love is carried to its ultimate possibilities, and sex and its high moments are transcended.

Sonnets

EDNA ST. VINCENT MILLAY

xxv

That Love at length should find me out and bring
This fierce and trivial brow unto the dust,
Is, after all, I must confess, but just;
There is a subtle beauty in this thing,
A wry perfection; wherefore now let sing
All voices how into my throat is thrust,
Unwelcome as Death's own, Love's bitter crust,

All criers proclaim it, and all steeples ring.
This being done, there let the matter rest.
What more remains is neither here nor there.
That you requite me not is plain to see;
Myself your slave herein have I confessed:
Thus far, indeed, the world may mock at me;
But if I suffer, it is my own affair.

xli
I, being born a woman and distressed
By all the needs and notions of my kind,
Am urged by your propinquity to find
Your person fair, and feel a certain zest
To bear your body's weight upon my breast:
So subtly is the fume of life designed,
To clarify the pulse and cloud the mind,
And leave me once again undone, possessed.
Think not for this, however, the poor treason
Of my stout blood against my staggering brain,
I shall remember you with love, or season
My scorn with pity,—let me make it plain:
I find this frenzy insufficient reason
For conversation when we meet again.

Nelly Trim

SYLVIA TOWNSEND WARNER

"Like men riding,
The mist from the sea
Drives down the valley
And baffles me."
"Enter, traveler,
Whoever you be."

By lamplight confronted
He staggered and peered;
Like a wet bramble
Was his beard.
"Sit down, stranger,
You look a-feared."

Shudders rent him
To the bone,
The wet ran off him
And speckled the stone.
"Dost bide here alone, maid?"
"Yes, alone."

As he sat down
In the chimney-nook
Over his shoulder
He cast a look,
As if the night
Were pursuing; she took

A handful of brash
To mend the fire,
He eyed her close
As the flame shot higher;
He spoke—and the cattle
Moved in the byre.

"Though you should heap
Your fire with wood,
'Twouldn't warm me
Nor do no good,
Unless you first warm me
As a maiden should."

With looks unwavering,
With breath unstirred,
She took off her clothes

Without a word,
And stood up naked
And white as a curd.

He breathed her to him
With famished sighs,
Against her bosom
He sheltered his eyes,
And warmed his hands
Between her thighs.

Strangely assembled
In the quiet room,
Alone alight
Amidst leagues of gloom,
So brave a bride,
So sad a groom;

And strange love-traffic
Between these two;
Nor mean, nor shamefaced—
As though they'd do
Something more solemn
Than they knew:

As though by this greeting
Which chance had willed
'Twixt him so silent
And her so stilled,
Some pledge or compact
Were fulfilled,

Made for all time
In times unknown,
'Twixt man and woman
Standing alone
In mirk night
By a tall stone.

His wayfaring terrors
All cast aside,
Brave now the bridegroom
Quitted the bride;
As he came, departing—
Undenied.

But once from darkness
Turned back his sight
To where in the doorway
She held a light:
"Good-by to you, maiden."
"Stranger, good night."

Long time has this woman
Been bedded alone.
The house where she slept
Lies stone on stone:
She'd not know her ash-tree,
So warped has it grown.

But yet this story
Is told of her
As a memorial;
And some aver
She'd comfort thus any
Poor traveler.

A wanton, you say—
Yet where's the spouse,
However true
To her marriage–vows,
To whom the lot
Of the earth-born allows

More than this?—
To comfort the care
Of a stranger, bound

She knows not where,
And afraid of the dark,
As his fathers were.

The Maid's Thought

ROBINSON JEFFERS

Why listen, even the water is sobbing for something.
The west wind is dead, the waves
Forget to hate the cliff, in the upland canyons
Whole hillsides burst aglow
With golden broom. Dear how it rained last month,
And every pool was rimmed
With sulphury pollen dust of the wakening pines.
Now tall and slender suddenly
The stalks of purple iris blaze by the brooks,
The penciled ones on the hill;
This deerweed shivers with gold, the white globe-tulips
Blow out their silky bubbles,
But in the next glen bronze-bells nod, the does
Scalded by some hot longing
Can hardly set their pointed hoofs to expect
Love but they crush a flower;
Shells pair on the rock, birds mate, the moths fly double.
O it is time for us now
Mouth kindling mouth to entangle our maiden bodies
To make that burning flower.

[from *Tulips and Chimneys*]

Sonnets

E. E. CUMMINGS

Realities ii
goodby Betty, don't remember me
pencil your eyes dear and have a good time
with the tall tight boys at Tabari'
s, keep your teeth snowy, stick to beer and lime,
wear dark, and where your meeting breasts are round
have roses darling, it's all i ask of you—
but that when light fails and this sweet profound
Paris moves with lovers, two and two
bound for themselves, when passionately dusk
brings softly down the perfume of the world
(and just as smaller stars begin to husk
heaven) you, you exactly paled and curled

with mystic lips take twilight where i know:
proving to Death that Love is so and so.

Actualities i
a thing most new complete fragile intense,
which wholly trembling memory undertakes
—your kiss, the little pushings of flesh, makes
my body sorry when the minute moon
is a remarkable splinter in the quick
of twilight
                    . . . . or if sunset utters one
unhurried muscled huge chromatic
fist skilfully modeling silence
—to feel how through the stopped entire day
horribly and seriously thrills
the moment of enthusiastic space
is a little wonderful, and say
Perhaps her body touched me; and to face

suddenly the lighted living hills

[from *The Divine Pilgrim*]

Lines from *The House of Dust*

CONRAD AIKEN

Part III, xii

Now, when the moon slid under the cloud
And the cold clear dark of starlight fell,
He heard in his blood the well-known bell
Tolling slowly in heaves of sound,
Slowly beating, slowly beating,
Shaking its pulse on the stagnant air:
Sometimes it swung completely round,
Horribly gasping as if for breath;
Falling down with an anguished cry . . .
Now the red bat, he mused, will fly;
Something is marked this night for death.

• • •

In the clear dark, on silent wings,
The red bat hovers beneath her moon;
She drops through the fragrant night, and clings
Fast in the shadow, with hands like claws,
With soft eyes closed and mouth that feeds,
To the young white flesh that warmly bleeds.
The maidens circle in dance, and raise
From lifting throats, a soft-sung praise;
Their knees and breasts are white and bare,
They have hung pale roses in their hair,
Each of them as she dances by
Peers at the blood with a narrowed eye.
See how the red wing wraps him round,
See how the white youth struggles in vain!
The weak arms writhe in a soundless pain;
He writhes in the soft red veiny wings,
But still she whispers upon him and clings.
This is the secret feast of love,
Look well, look well, before it dies,

See how the red one trembles above,
See how quiet the white one lies!   .   .   .

.   .   .

Dance! Dance! Dance! Dance!
Dance till the brain is red with speed!
Dance till you fall! Lift your torches!
Kiss your lovers until they bleed!
Backward I press you until you cry,
Until your eyes are stretched with pain;
Backward I press you until you cry,
Your lips grow white, I kiss you again,
I will take a torch and set you afire,
I will break your body and fling it away.   .   .   .
Look, you are trembling.   .   .   .   Lie still, beloved!
Lock your hands in my hair, and say
Darling! darling! darling! darling!
All night long till the break of day.

.   .   .

The great bell cracks and falls at last.
The moon whirls out. The sky grows still.
Look, how the white cloud crosses the stars
And suddenly drops behind the hill!
Your eyes are placid, you smile at me,
We sit in the room by candle-light.
We peer in each other's veins and see
No sign of the things we saw this night.
Only, a song is in your ears,
A song you have heard, you think, in dream:
The song which only the demon hears,
In the dark forest where maenads scream   .   .   .

'By the clear waters where once I died   .   .   .
In the calm evening bright with stars   .   .   .'
What do the strange words mean? you say,—
And touch my hand, and turn away.

Lines from *Roan Stallion*

ROBINSON JEFFERS

      It was like daylight
Out-doors and she hastened without faltering down the foot-
    path, through the dark fringe of twisted oak-brush,
To the open place in a bay of the hill. The dark strength of
    the stallion had heard her coming; she heard him
Blow the shining air out of his nostrils, she saw him in the
    white lake of moonlight
Move like a lion along the timbers of the fence, shaking the
    nightfall
Of the great mane; his fragrance came to her; she leaned on
    the fence;
He drew away from it, the hooves making soft thunder in the
    trodden soil.
Wild love had trodden it, his wrestling with the stranger, the
    shame of the day
Had stamped it into mire and powder when the heavy fetlocks
Strained the soft flanks. "Oh, if I could bear you!
If I had the strength. O great God that came down to
    Mary, gently you came. But I will ride him
Up into the hill, if he throws me, if he tramples me, is it not
    my desire
To endure death?" She climbed the fence, pressing her body
    against the rail, shaking like fever,
And dropped inside to the soft ground. He neither threat-
    ened her with his teeth nor fled from her coming,
And lifting her hand gently to the upflung head she caught
    the strap of the headstall,
That hung under the quivering chin. She unlooped the halter
    from the high strength of the neck
And the arch the storm-cloud mane hung with live darkness.
    He stood; she crushed her breasts
On the hard shoulder, an arm over the withers, the other
    under the mass of his throat, and murmuring

Like a mountain dove, "If I could bear you." No way, no
    help, a gulf in nature. She murmured, "Come,
We will run on the hill. O beautiful, O beautiful," and led
    him
To the gate and flung the bars on the ground. He threw
    his head downward
To snuff at the bars; and while he stood, she catching mane
    and withers with all sudden contracture
And strength of her lithe body, leaped, clung hard, and was
    mounted. He had been ridden before; he did not
Fight the weight but ran like a stone falling;
Broke down the slope into the moon-glass of the stream, and
    flattened to his neck
She felt the branches of a buck-eye tree fly over her, saw
    the wall of the oak-scrub
End her world: but he turned there, the matted branches
Scraped her right knee, the great slant shoulders
Laboring the hill-slope, up, up, the clear hill. Desire had
    died in her
At the first rush, the falling like death, but now it revived,
She feeling between her thighs the labor of the great engine,
    the running muscles, the hard swiftness,
She riding the savage and exultant strength of the world.
    Having topped the thicket he turned eastward,
Running less wildly; and now at length he felt the halter
    when she drew on it; she guided him upward;
He stopped and grazed on the great arch and pride of the
    hill, the silent calvary. A dwarfish oakwood
Climbed the other slope out of the dark of the unknown
    canyon beyond; the last wind-beaten bush of it
Crawled up to the height, and California slipping from her
    mount tethered him to it. She stood then,
Shaking. Enormous films of moonlight
Trailed down from the height. Space, anxious whiteness,
    vastness. Distant beyond conception the shining ocean
Lay light like a haze along the ledge and doubtful world's
    end. Little vapors gleaming, and little

Darknesses on the far chart underfoot symbolized wood and
    valley; but the air was the element, the moon—
Saturate arcs and spires of the air.
                  Here is solitude, here on the
    calvary, nothing conscious
But the possible God and the cropped grass, no witness, no
    eye but that misformed one, the moon's past fullness.
Two figures on the shining hill, woman and stallion, she
    kneeling to him, brokenly adoring.
He cropping the grass, shifting his hooves, or lifting the long
    head to gaze over the world,
Tranquil and powerful. She prayed aloud, "O God I am
    not good enough, O fear, O strength, I am draggled.
Johnny and other men have had me, and O clean power!
    Here am I," she said, falling before him,
And crawled to his hooves. She lay a long while, as if
    asleep, in reach of the fore-hooves, weeping. He avoided
Her head and the prone body. He backed at first; but later
    plucked the grass that grew by her shoulder.
The small dark head under his nostrils: a small round stone,
    that smelt human, black hair growing from it:
The skull shut the light in: it was not possible for any eyes
To know what throbbed and shone under the sutures of the
    skull, or a shell full of lightning
Had scared the roan strength, and he'd have broken tether,
    screaming, and run for the valley.
                    The atom bounds-breaking,
Nucleus to sun, electrons to planets, with recognition
Not praying, self-equaling, the whole to the whole, the
    microcosm
Not entering nor accepting entrance, more equally, more ut-
    terly, more incredibly conjugate
With the other extreme and greatness; passionately percep-
    tive of identity. . . .
            The fire threw up figures
And symbols meanwhile, racial myths formed and dissolved
    in it, the phantom rulers of humanity

That without being are yet more real than what they are
     born of, and without shape, shape that which makes them:
The nerves and the flesh go by shadowlike, the limbs and the
     lives shadowlike, these shadows remain, these shadows
To whom temples, to whom churches, to whom labors and
     wars, visions and dreams are dedicate:
Out of the fire in the small round stone that black moss cov-
     ered, a crucified man writhed up in anguish;
A woman covered by a huge beast in whose mane the stars
     were netted, sun and moon were his eyeballs,
Smiled under the unendurable violation, her throat swollen
     with the storm and blood-flecks gleaming
On the stretched lips; a woman—no, a dark water, split by
     jets of lightning, and after a season
What floated up out of the furrowed water, a boat, a fish, a
     fire-globe?
                 It had wings, the creature,
And flew against the fountain of lightning, fell burnt out of
     the cloud back to the bottomless water . . .
Figures and symbols, castlings of the fire, played in her
     brain; but the white fire was the essence,
The burning in the small round shell of bone that black hair
     covered, that lay by the hooves on the hilltop.

She rose at length, she unknotted the halter; she walked and
     led the stallion; two figures, woman and stallion,
Came down the silent emptiness of the dome of the hill, under
     the cataract of the moonlight.

Lines from *Tristram*

EDWIN ARLINGTON ROBINSON

. . . . Softly, behind him,
The coming of her steps had made him turn
To see there was no fear in her eyes now;

And whether she had come to him from death,
Or through those dark and heavy velvet curtains,
She had come to him silent and alone,
And as the living come—living or not.
Whether it was a warm ghost he was holding,
Or a warm woman, or a dream of one,
With tear-filled eyes in a slow twilight shining
Upward and into his, only to leave him
With eyes defeated of all sight of her,
Was more than he dared now let fate reveal.
Whatever it was that he was holding there,
Woman or ghost or dream, was not afraid;
And the warm lips that pressed themselves again
On his, and held them there as if to die there,
Were not dead now. The rest might be illusion—
Camelot, Arthur, Guinevere, Gawaine,
Lancelot, and that voyage with Lancelot
To Joyous Gard, this castle by the sea—
The sea itself, and the clouds over it,
Like embers of a day that like a city
Far off somewhere in time was dying alone,
Slowly, in fire and silence—the fading light
Around them, and the shadowy room that held them—
All these,—if they were shadows, let them be so,
He thought. But let these two that were not shadows
Be as they were, and live—by time no more
Divided until time for them should cease.
They were not made for time as others were,
And time therefore would not be long for them
Wherein for love to learn that in their love,
Where fate was more than time and more than love,
Time never was, save in their fear of it—
Fearing, as one, to find themselves again
Intolerably as two that were not there.

.   .   .

.   .   .   .   Stronger than God,
When all was done the god of love was fate,

Where all was love. And this was in a darkness
Where time was always dying and never dead,
And where God's face was never to be seen
To tell the few that were to lose the world
For love how much or little they lost for it,
Or paid with others' pain.

✿ BEAUTY

CHRISTOPHER LAFARGE / *Honeysuckle*

EDNA ST. VINCENT MILLAY / *Sonnets xxx and xliii*

JAMES RORTY / *Copan*

EDWIN ARLINGTON ROBINSON / Lines from *Rembrandt to Rembrandt*

WALLACE STEVENS / Lines from *It Must Be Abstract* (from *Notes Toward A Supreme Fiction*)

RAYMOND HOLDEN / *The Poet*

HILDEGARDE FLANNER / *Driving Clock*

{§} *Although identified theoretically with the doctrine of self-*expression, the elevation of beauty to the status of a principle aim of existence was the one positive contribution of the twenties toward the accumulation of a new culture to replace the one its Lost Generation had swept away. In *Honeysuckle*, Christopher LaFarge, exquisite classical lyricist, gives us elemental, pagan, sensuous beauty, at first objective, but at the end very delicately merging into sensuality, identifying its period. In the two sonnets given here, Millay likewise moves between ideal classical beauty, objective sensuous beauty, and, again speaking for the period, the intimate association between creative art and sex.

In *Copan*, James Rorty, his talent as always directed by "Social Consciousness" more typical of the thirties than of the twenties, gives us the classical idea of art, permanent as the earth, looking down on the vanishing generations of men. Rorty is one of the three poets the greatness of whose perceptions compels their inclusion in this book, in spite of occasional lapses into rhetorical prose.

In *Rembrandt to Rembrandt*, Robinson celebrates talent and the exercise of it as predestined, perforce to be practiced irrespective of success or failure. Incidentally, he comments on the meaninglessness of critical fashion.

In their two poems given here, Stevens and Holden, using a slightly different vocabulary, both celebrate with infinite delicacy aesthetic perception as revealing absolute, inexpressible reality.

In the very great poem *Driving Clock*, Hildegarde Flanner introduces us to the new world of technology and its aesthetic, celebrating the beauty of the machine as identical with the truth of the mysterious cosmos.

Honeysuckle

CHRISTOPHER LA FARGE

There in hot darkness was a zone so sweet
I could not follow
God's beaten path and hollow,

But let my treacherous and my wandered feet
From paths retreat.

Of still and yellow chalices there arose
On maenad air
The lust of love's despair
Black blazing in fit darkness to disclose
What days oppose.

Caught in each horn elixir's music hung
In scented notes,
The pagan passionate throats
Sang in the night and in the Doric tongue:
Still, still be young!

O clear and Christian God, how may you say
I did not right
When on this summer's night
In the great pagan splendor of delay
I left your way?

Sonnets

EDNA ST. VINCENT MILLAY

xxx

Sometimes when I am wearied suddenly
Of all the things that are the outward you,
And my gaze wanders ere your tale is through
To webs of my own weaving, or I see
Abstractedly your hands about your knee
And wonder why I love you as I do,
Then I recall, "Yet *Sorrow* thus he drew";
Then I consider, "*Pride* thus painted he."
Oh, friend, forget not, when you fain would note

In me a beauty that was never mine,
How first you knew me in a book I wrote,
How first you loved me for a written line:
So are we bound till broken is the throat
Of Song, and Art no more leads out the Nine.

xliii
Still will I harvest beauty where it grows:
In coloured fungus and the spotted fog
Surprised on foods forgotten; in ditch and bog
Filmed brilliant with irregular rainbows
Of rust and oil, where half a city throws
Its empty tins; and in some spongy log
Whence headlong leaps the oozy emerald frog. . . .
And a black pupil in the green scum shows.
Her the inhabiter of divers places
Surmising at all doors, I push them all.
Oh, you that fearful of a creaking hinge
Turn back forevermore with craven faces,
I tell you Beauty bears an ultra fringe
Unguessed of you upon her gossamer shawl!

Copan

JAMES RORTY

Did you hear when our plane was dropped
Like a loud question into the lost
Silence of this parched and windless valley?
Did you hear, O High Priest? Now . . . do you hear?

I hear. What sleeps here lives more fiercely still
Despite its noise, than that improbable
Sorcerer's hawk you ride in . . . Yes, I hear.

When did you fall, and how?
Was it dogma or doubt? Did the slaves
Revolt, or the clerks betray? Did the priest,
Plucking the slack string of fear, get instead
An arrow in the back? Or did the slow
Blood-drip turning to lava on the stone
Make foul the temple whence the gods had gone?

There was never blood enough. The slaves
Craved it, or so we thought. Always they wanted
More, more . . .   The stretched victim, the dripping heart
Wrenched from the breast, the smeared god, and then
Always the vile crowd's jaguar-howl when the flung carcass
Rolled down the stair, the priest dancing . . .

You danced?

We danced. Always the priest must dance.
Do you not dance, you who come prying
Here at the grave of power, to be outstared
By these, our ordered agonies of stone? What
Doubt besets you? Do you fear now
Your godlessness as we feared once
Tepecu and Gucumatz and Hurucan,
The Heart of Heaven?

Charlatan! We have found the priest's
Secret chamber. We have found the long tube reaching
To the god's mouth. Liar and cheat! What price
To the starveling artist who sculped
The despot's gentle lips, his visioned brow?
Ten centuries have passed, and still these ruins
Are crusted with the sweat of fools, the blood
Of twice ten million slaves.

What then? They were plant-simple and dog-dirty.
Bound to the earth and to themselves. We gave them

Prayer, and gods to pray to, Tepecu,
And Gucumatz, and Hurucan, the Heart
Of Heaven; priests to fear and serve;
Sacrificers to sate their blood-lust, art,
Roads to build and tall white cities, games,
Star-knowledge, the measured depth of time; a share
In our Mayan glory, until . . .

Until what? Was it famine or plague?
The blight of war, or the earth's decline?
Speak, priest, the secret!

. . . Until the serpent's mouth swallowed us, the stone
Jaguar leapt from his pedestal and fled
Howling to the jungle, the slaves
Ran back to their milpas in the hills. You make
Mysteries where none is. Art is for art's
Sake, and power for power's. We tired of our small
Blood-lettings, tired of fearing and being feared:
Tired of our small toys as you will tire
Of your great ones. Nothing lasts, but art
Lasts longest. How many million slaves
Piled these stones? . . . We do not know; that count
We lost, but the stones remain, and the fear
In the stone eyes of the priest, and the spread
Jaws of the serpent, and overhead
The slow procession of the stars.

Lines from *Rembrandt to Rembrandt*

EDWIN ARLINGTON ROBINSON

And there's a Rembrandt to be satisfied
Who never will be, howsoever much
He be assured of an ascendancy

That has not yet a shadow's worth of sound
Where Holland has its ears. And what of that?

.   .   .

You are the servant, Rembrandt, not the master,—
But you are not assigned with other slaves
That in their freedom are the most in fear.
One of the few that are so fortunate
As to be told their task and to be given
A skill to do it with a tool too keen
For timid safety, bow your elected head
Under the stars tonight, and whip your devils
Each to his nest in hell.

.   .   .

                Nor more are you
In any sudden danger to forget
That in Apollo's house there are no clocks
Or calendars to say for you in time
How far you are away from Amsterdam,
Or that the one same law that bids you see
Where now you see alone forbids in turn
Your light from Holland eyes till Holland ears
Are told of it; for that way, my good fellow,
Is one way more to death. If at the first
Of your long turning, which may still be longer
Than even your faith has measured it, you sigh
For distant welcome that may not be seen,
Or wayside shouting that will not be heard,
You may as well accommodate your greatness
To the convenience of an easy ditch,
And, anchored there with all your widowed gold,
Forget your darkness in the dark, and hear
No longer the cold wash of Holland scorn.

[from *Notes Toward
A Supreme Fiction*]

Lines from *It Must Be Abstract*

WALLACE STEVENS

iii

The poem refreshes life so that we share,
For a moment, the first idea   .   .   .   It satisfies
Belief in an immaculate beginning

And sends us, winged by an unconscious will,
To an immaculate end. We move between these
   points:
From that ever-early candor to its late plural

And the candor of them is the strong exhilaration
Of what we feel from what we think, of thought
Beating in the heart, as if blood newly came,

.   .   .

iv

The first idea was not our own.   Adam
In Eden was the father of Descartes
And Eve made air the mirror of herself,

.   .   .

From this the poem springs: that we live in a place
That is not our own and, much more, not ourselves
And hard it is in spite of blazoned days.

.   .   .

The Poet

RAYMOND HOLDEN

It is a larger thing I see
Than at the moment I confront:
The daylight, bent away from me,
The daylight welling from its font
And all the shadows that are things
Possessed and lost and not conceived,
Stopped in their widespread shadowings
Sharp as the scallop umbrage leaved
At simple noon by trees on walks.
It is the maker and his mark,
The shape and heart of all that talks,
The cup of light, the liquid dark.

It is a wider thing I know
That I can pile upon a hand:
The sense of having lived to grow
In many a visitless strange land
Where all that happens is to come
And all that's hoped is memory;
Where every stick and stone's a home
And every home a stone or tree,
And all that ripples from a lip
Into the ear-attended air
Is but a reaching fingertip
Of one in darkness on a stair.   ·

It is a worthier thing I am
Than this I draw my breath to be:
A mesh of loop and length to cram
With meaning, meaningless to me
Unless it strike the ringing throat
And break to symbols, outward bound,
Suggesting by some broken note
The logic ancestry of sound.

Larger and wider, worthier
Than I, this tongue no man was taught.
I speak, and over speech's stir
Hear the great silence taking thought.

Driving Clock

HILDEGARDE FLANNER

(Below Mt. Wilson Observatory)

Lovely wheel that weds along the groove
And wedless parts the shimmer of your rim
To silver singly in the tempered air,
You, slow as God, have overtaken Him.

Pale perimeter of grace, anointed
For that hypnotic glide impinged on might,
Who forged you on the anvil of the stars
And set you turning to the laws of light?

How cryptic is the calm, the intricate
Unindolence of power that knows its place,
So gravely balanced between pole and pole,
So local in the mystery of space.

Time is a solid here, co-bound and wrought
With matter's destiny. Tell, who can tell
How period is lapped in pause of steel,
How truth is made to fit itself so well?

✿ LOVE

✿ *In this section there is little that is peculiar to the twenties*, unless an implication by four of the seven poets that love was usually frustrate in an age that was trying to deny it by identifying it with sex.

In *My Light with Yours*, Edgar Lee Masters records, with less overwriting than is his habit, the timelessness and placelessness of love.

In *Night Song at Amalfi*, Sara Teasdale laments the inability of woman to express her love. Here, as rarely, Teasdale rises above the transcription of personal experience and attains universal statement.

In the passage from *Tristram* we have the final defeat of romantic love without the benefit of mystical adjustment. Isolt of the White Hands was not equipped with the feminism of the twenties. Her love, instead of struggling for defiant independence, is settling into high sentimentality and will live henceforth on its own sweetness.

With no comparable work I know of except the *Sonnets from the Portuguese*, VanDoren's sonnet series is a record of realized, lifelong love, and as such on the part of a man it is perhaps unique in great poetry in English. More profoundly if less exclusively passionate, it suggests comparison with Elinor Wylie's great series which also speaks with the tone and intention of permanence.

The juxtaposition of Wylie's love sonnets with Millay's two sonnets of renunciation throws into contrast the two women of the twenties with the best claim to admission to the small list (about a dozen) of the world's greatest poets. Both were essentially romantic, tending to celebrate perfect experience that is not fully realized; but Wylie, as in these sonnets, is farther in the classical direction. She records experience that is either present or immediately in prospect, whereas Millay usually tells of experience that is either hopeless, imperfect, or, as in the two sonnets here, is past and gone. Wylie's technique is compact, precise, tightly polished and glittering; Millay's is more spontaneous, more diffuse and expansive. Wylie sometimes falls into that rationalized, conscious composition which is always the threat hanging over classical writing; Millay sometimes crosses the line into the direct transcription of experience which is one danger of romanticism. Wylie's greatness, in the sonnets that follow, and in the few other places where she approaches it, is in depth, in passion at once circumscribed and as profound as humanity can attain. Millay's greatness is in width and height. In contrast to Wylie's tropes chiseled into perfect aptness, Millay's allegories and metaphors unexpectedly unveil universal vistas, as it were, without effort. At the end of each of her sonnets that close this section, after thirteen lines of merely facile excellence, suddenly in the final line the poetic curtain whips up on all there is to know of human tragedy.

My Light With Yours

EDGAR LEE MASTERS

i

When the sea has devoured the ships,
And the spires and the towers
Have gone back to the hills.
And all the cities
Are one with the plains again.
And the beauty of bronze,
And the strength of steel
Are blown over silent continents,
As the desert sand is blown—
My dust with yours forever.

ii

When folly and wisdom are no more,
And fire is no more,
Because man is no more;
When the dead world slowly spinning
Drifts and falls through the void—
My light with yours
In the Light of Lights forever!

Night Song at Amalfi

SARA TEASDALE

I asked the heaven of stars
    What I should give my love—
It answered me with silence,
    Silence above.

I asked the darkened sea
    Down where the fishers go—
It answered me with silence,
    Silence below.

Oh, I could give him weeping,
    Or I could give him song—
But how can I give silence,
    My whole life long?

Lines from *Tristram*

EDWIN ARLINGTON ROBINSON

              Isolt of the white hands,
Isolt with her gray eyes and her white face,
Still gazed across the water to the north
But not now for a ship. Were ships to come,
No fleet of them could hold a golden cargo
That would be worth one agate that was hers—
One toy that he had given her long ago,
And long ago forgotten. Yet there she gazed
Across the water, over the white waves,
Upon a castle that she had never seen,
And would not see, save as a phantom shape
Against a phantom sky. He had been there,

She thought, but not with her. He had died there,
But not for her. He had not thought of her,
Perhaps, and that was strange. He had been all,
And would be always all there was for her,
And he had not come back to her alive,
Not even to go again. It was like that
For women, sometimes, and might be so too often
For women like her. She hoped there were not many
Of them, or many of them to be, not knowing
More about that than about waves and foam,
And white birds everywhere, flying, and flying;
Alone, with her white face and her gray eyes,
She watched them there till even her thoughts were white,
And there was nothing alive but white birds flying,
Flying, and always flying, and still flying,
And the white sunlight flashing on the sea.

Sonnets

MARK VAN DOREN

i

I said: It will not blow this way again;
The branches of my life too soon are old;
The wind is kind to early-withered men
Lest they remember and confess the cold.
I said, and scarcely knew that it was I,
Hanging my leaves there in the springless year.
I said; and did not listen to a high,
Loud sound of March that filled the woods with fear.
Then it was all around me, till at last
Love like a hurricane of hate was blowing,
Bruising me everywhere. Yet I was fast,
And stood among the ruins of his going.

Only the after stillness came and showed
These blossoms on me everywhere, like blood.

ii

No wonder-deed done in the oldest time
Whose whiteness burns oblivion away,
No miracle of grass, whose muted rhyme
Outsings the dawn and silences the jay,
No fiend's invention, no good man's endeavor,
No other tale of love is so untrue
As this one of my heart, that empties never,
But fills even as you take, and still is new.
It cannot be there is more love to come;
Yet, coming on, love tells me I have lied.
So I must learn to listen and grow dumb,
Believing in a heart that never died:
    Believing then in you, who like a dream
    Draw out of me this ever waking stream.

viii

When I am called by Love to give account
Of the one thing that holds me unto you,
I will obey him to the strict amount;
One nameless thing I know, and it must do.
I will tell Love how first you looked at me:
Head down, and something level in your eyes;
How still you stood and looked; and I could see
Half-risen modesty, to rule surprise;
How then you spoke, and how your voice was low,
And how your arms hung perfectly await.
I will ask Love himself to pause and go,
And look, and understand my changeless state:
    Rooted again within your level gaze,
    Eternal now across the evening ways.

ix

All of the steps that our slow love has taken
Were your own steps at last, who led the way.

I was too fixed—or like an oak was shaken
That has been marked to fall yet never may.
Never unless you taught me had I known it:
Love must be advancing or it dies.
You found each resting-place, but had outgrown it
Before I too was ready to arise.
Love is a journey to no end, except
One traveller, halting, cannot journey more.
When I awoke you had as wisely stepped
As the sole fox across a forest floor;
   So I would always follow you; and will
   To the last hedge upon the highest hill.

xvii

When I came back to your unlifted eyes,
And spoke to you, inquiring how we did,
And you looked up without the least surmise—
Then the old music, that so long was hid,
Sounded; and I knew it was to pour
Forever while we lived, with no abating.
The unskilled players were unskilled no more,
And every string had sweetened by its waiting.
There will be nothing now but one clear tone,
Of which we shall not tire; and when it pauses
We shall exist upon love's faith alone,
That knows all silence to its deepest causes;
   And comprehends the ever devious ways
   I still must follow as I sing your praise.

xviii

I would dislike you if you used an art
To make me love you more than this, the most;
For it is only downward that the heart
Could move from such an eminence. Poor boast!
Each day I am confounded, for you give
Each day the wheel of love a little turn;
And I go headlong with it, lest I live
Henceforth one arc behind; and never learn

There is no going downward in our love;
I could not fall and lose you if I tried.
There is no under here, and no above,
But round and round; and distances have died.
  Nor am I ever giddy, for love's air,
  Like this of earth, turns with it everywhere.

xx

Let it be always secret what we say;
And where we meet, be that our world alone.
Nor think us ever guilty, since our day
Is one on which no shadowbands have shown.
Shame is a shadow that will never fall
On us who have cut down the trees of pride.
Let the world darken past the garden wall;
The space within is conscienceless and wide.
Nor think us ever weary, or in need
Of company to bring the night at last.
Love is a lonely and contented deed,
Done in a desert that is sweet and vast;
  Where neither of us turns a timeless head
  To see the world behind us that is dead.

xxviii

Never to be renewed or to increase,
And never to be changed from what it was:
The love that was the maker of this lease
Was love-upon-first-sight, whom all the laws
Of happiness obey, and kingdoms coming
Choose to be the glory of their thrones.
He is the oldest love, he is the humming
Of these incessant bees among my bones;
He is the senses' king; my youngest thought
He molds before I know it has been born;
He is the flesh's despot; the inwrought,
Deep joy; or in my side the sudden thorn.
  Oh, strange that on that day I was so strong,
  Bearing him all at once; and now so long!

xxxii

Not pride it was that made me say so much
Bearing on my own mind in these, your songs.
Intended for your praise, they did but touch
Idea, where your beauty best belongs,
And straightway thought was active, bringing proof,
Here in my heart's possession, of your power.
These but effects; the cause remains aloof;
There is no certain entrance to the tower.
If any gate were open I would climb,
Life-long, and reach your verity at last;
And sing—Oh, I can hear the happy rhyme
Break upward, I can see the overcast
   Part swiftly, and can lose the final sound.
   Alas! I never heard it from this ground.

xxxiii

My only need—you ask me, and I tell you—
Is that henceforth forever you exist.
You are not mine; I may not ever bell you
Like an owned animal for night and mist.
My only need, whatever darkness take me,
Whatever tears close now my separate eyes,
Is that you live, and let the knowledge make me
Immortal as the day that never dies—
That, swift and even, turns into the sun,
As turns the aftershadow down to death.
Let neither then my night, my day be done;
Let them both swing in silence, with no breath
   To call you from the distances you keep.
   Would they were little; would that my love could sleep.

Sonnets

ELINOR WYLIE

i

Now shall the long homesickness have an end
Upon your heart, which is a part of all
The past no human creature may recall
Save you, who are persuasive to unbend
The brows of death, and name him for a friend;
This ecstasy is supernatural;
I have survived to see the heavens fall
Into my hands, which on your hands depend.

Time has prepared us an enduring bed
Within the earth of this beloved land;
And, lying side by side and hand in hand,
We sleep coeval with the happy dead
Who are ourselves, a little earlier bound
To one another's bosom in the ground.

ii

What other name had half expressed the whole
Of that incomparable and touching grace
Which spells the shape of danger in your face?
It is the very pattern of your soul;
The eagle's home, above the moon's control,
Above the seas, the high precipitate place;
The stairway cut from planetary space;
The crystal steps which climb a steeper goal.

The shadow of its light is only this:
That all your beauty is the work of wars
Between the upper and the nether stars;
Its symmetry is perfect and severe
Because the barbarous force of agonies
Broke it, and mended it, and made it clear.

v

The little beauty that I was allowed—
The lips new-cut and coloured by my sire,
The polished hair, the eyes' perceptive fire—
Has never been enough to make me proud:
For I have moved companioned by a cloud,
And lived indifferent to the blood's desire
Of temporal loveliness in vain attire:
My flesh was but a fresh-embroidered shroud.

Now do I grow indignant at the fate
Which made me so imperfect to compare
With your degree of noble and of fair;
Our elements are the farthest skies apart;
And I enjoin you, ere it is too late,
To stamp your superscription on my heart.

vi

I have believed that I prefer to live
Preoccupied by a Platonic mind;
I have believed me obdurate and blind
To those sharp ecstasies the pulses give:
The clever body five times sensitive
I never have discovered to be kind
As the poor soul, deceived and half-divined,
Whose hopes are water in a witch's sieve.

O now both soul and body are unfit
To apprehend this miracle, my lord!
Not all my senses, striving in accord
With my pure essence, are aware of it
Save as a power remote and exquisite,
Not seen or known, but fervently adored.

x

When I perceive the sable of your hair
Silvered, and deep within those caverns are
Your eyesockets, a double-imaged star,

And your fine substance fretted down by care,
Then do I marvel that a woman dare
Prattle of mortal matters near and far
To one so wounded in demonic war
Against some prince of Sirius or Altair.

How is it possible that this hand of clay,
Though white as porcelain, can contrive a touch
So delicate it shall not hurt too much?
What voice can my invention find to say
So soft, precise, and scrupulous a word
You shall not take it for another sword?

xiv

My fairer body and perfected spirit,
Beyond metempsychosis, and beyond
The faults you must forgive me to be fond,
Are yours in any death that I may merit;
Mortality has wearied us who wear it,
And they are wiser creatures who have shunned
This miry world, this slough of man's despond,
To fortify the skies we shall inherit.

I have entreated you to grant me Time
To memorize the pure appointed task;
Today it is Eternity I ask
In which to learn the lesson of this rhyme:
Its liberal periods are not too wide
To educate me fitly for your bride.

xvi

I hereby swear that to uphold your house
I would lay my bones in quick destroying lime
Or turn my flesh to timber for all time;
Cut down my womanhood; lop off the boughs
Of that perpetual ecstasy that grows
From the heart's core; condemn it as a crime
If it be broader than a beam, or climb
Above the stature that your roof allows.

I am not the hearthstone nor the cornerstone
Within this noble fabric you have builded;
Not by my beauty was its cornice gilded;
Not on my courage were its arches thrown:
My lord, adjudge my strength, and set me where
I bear a little more than I can bear.

xviii
Let us leave talking of angelic hosts
Of nebulae, and lunar hemispheres,
And what the days, and what the Uranian years
Shall offer us when you and I are ghosts;
Forget the festivals and pentecosts
Of metaphysics, and the lesser fears
Confound us, and seal up our eyes and ears
Like little rivers locked below the frosts.

And let us creep into the smallest room
That any hunted exile has desired
For him and for his love when he was tired;
And sleep oblivious of any doom
Which is beyond our reason to conceive;
And so forget to weep, forget to grieve,
And wake, and touch each other's hands, and turn
Upon a bed of juniper and fern.

Sonnets

EDNA ST. VINCENT MILLAY

cxi
O ailing Love, compose your struggling wing!
Confess you mortal; be content to die.
How better dead, than be this awkward thing
Dragging in dust its feathers of the sky,

Hitching and rearing, plunging beak to loam,
Upturned, disheveled, utt'ring a weak sound
Less proud than of the gull that rakes the foam,
Less kind than of the hawk that scours the ground.
While yet your awful beauty, even at bay,
Beats off the impious eye, the outstretched hand,
And what your hue or fashion none can say,
Vanish, be fled, leave me a wingless land   .   .   .
Save where one moment down the quiet tide
Fades a white swan, with a black swan beside.

cxvii
Now by the path I climbed, I journey back.
The oaks have grown; I have been long away.
Taking with me your memory and your lack
I now descend into a milder day;
Stripped of your love, unburdened of my hope,
Descend the path I mounted from the plain;
Yet steeper than I fancied seems the slope
And stonier, now that I go down again.
Warm falls the dusk; the clanking of a bell
Faintly ascends upon this heavier air;
I do recall those grassy pastures well:
In early spring they drove the cattle there.
And close at hand should be a shelter, too,
From which the mountain peaks are not in view.

❁ VISTAS

ROBERT FROST / *Once by the Pacific* / Lines from *I Will Sing You One-O*

E. E. CUMMINGS / *Impressions, iv* (from *Tulips and Chimneys*)

BABETTE DEUTSCH / Lines from *Epistle to Prometheus*

CHARD POWERS SMITH / Lines from *The Fourth God* (from *Prelude to Man*)

ARCHIBALD MACLEISH / *You, Andrew Marvell*

WALLACE STEVENS / Lines from *The Auroras of Autumn*

❀ *These are poems or passages whose aura of greatness arises* chiefly from the magnificence of the physical scene. Equally or more magnificent are scenes presented in other sections, from Crane's *The Bridge*, Jeffers's *Cawdor*, MacLeish's *Epistle to be Left in the Earth*, LaFarge's *Mercy by Night*, and Robinson's *As It Looked Then*. But in those, the greatness of the scene is lost in some other greatness, human or ideational. In each of the poems that follow either the scene is larger than the human content or it is essential to the size of the human content.

In Frost's early poem, *Once by the Pacific*, there is an apocalyptic overtone, but it is negligible in contemplation of the sheer power of the marine spectacle. In *I Will Sing You One-O* his playfulness in technique sometimes replaces the poetry, but the cosmic panorama remains.

In Cummings's *impressions, iv*, the subject of the poem is the brutality of the city, but it takes its universality from the grandeur of the sky.

Babette Deutsch's comment on humanity, if reduced to prose, would not be original. But the grandeur of the spectacle in which it is dramatized gives it a sense of tremendous originality.

In my epic of evolution, the perpetual large vista is in time rather than space. In the passage excerpted here, from near the end of the poem, I hope the temporal sweep is combined with a sufficiently impressive spatial one.

In MacLeish's *You, Andrew Marvell*, the hopelessness is lost in the magnificent shadow coming on—c. p. Housman's "towering foolscap of eternal shade."

The Auroras of Autumn, with its palette of pale, exotic colors shimmering in the Northern Lights—cool greens, cold blues, white, bronze, sometimes a shaft of gold or purple, all the half seen colors of thought—provide a suitable setting for all of Stevens's work.

Once by the Pacific
ROBERT FROST

The shattered water made a misty din.
Great waves looked over others coming in,
And thought of doing something to the shore
That water never did to land before.
The clouds were low and hairy in the skies,
Like locks blown forward in the gleam of eyes.
You could not tell, and yet it looked as if
The shore was lucky in being backed by cliff,
The cliff in being backed by continent;
It looked as if a night of dark intent
Was coming, and not only a night, an age.
Someone had better be prepared for rage.
There would be more than ocean-water broken
Before God's last *Put out the Light* was spoken.

Lines From *I Will Sing You One-O*
ROBERT FROST

The tower said, "One!"
And then a steeple.
They spoke to themselves
And such few people
As winds might rouse
From sleeping warm
(But not unhouse).
They left the storm
That struck *en masse*
My window glass
Like a beaded fur.
In that grave One

They spoke of the sun
And moon and stars,
Saturn and Mars
And Jupiter.
Still more unfettered,
They left the named
And spoke of the lettered,
The sigmas and taus
Of constellations.
They filled their throats
With the furthest bodies
To which man sends his
Speculation,
Beyond which God is;
The cosmic motes
Of yawning lenses.
Their solemn peals
Were not their own:
They spoke for the clock
With whose vast wheels
Theirs interlock.
In that grave word
Uttered alone
The utmost star
Trembled and stirred,
Though set so far
Its whirling frenzies
Appear like standing
In one self station.
It has not ranged,
And save for the wonder
Of once expanding
To be a nova,
It has not changed
To the eye of man
On planets over
Around and under
It in creation

Since man began
To drag down man
And nation nation.

[from *Tulips and Chimneys*]

Impressions

E. E. CUMMINGS

iv

The hours rise up putting off stars and it is
dawn
into the street of the sky light walks scattering poems

on earth a candle is
extinguished   the city
wakes
with a song upon her
mouth having death in her eyes

and it is dawn
the world
goes forth to murder dreams . . . .

i see in the street where strong
men are digging bread
and i see the brutal faces of
people contented hideous hopeless cruel happy

and it is day,

in the mirror
i see a frail
man
dreaming

dreams
dreams in the mirror

and it
is dusk   on earth

a candle is lighted . . . .
and it is dark.
the people are in their houses
the frail man is in his bed
the city

sleeps with death upon her mouth having a song in her eyes
the hours descend,
putting on stars . . . .

in the street of the sky night walks scattering poems

Lines from *Epistle to Prometheus*

BABETTE DEUTSCH

How beautiful upon the mountains are the feet of him
    that bringeth good tidings, that publisheth peace.
But your feet, prisoner of Zeus,
the gyves made angry,
upon the mountains where they stretched you,
who had brought
not peace to earth,
but fire.

There are ranges
so tall they nuzzle Space,
but no man dare
climb to their lips.
You alone, Titan, were a morsel fit

for virgin tusks
to tear.
Ah, how they tasted you with tongues of ice!
breathed on you hoarsely from their windy gorges!
how, like a fire too nice,
licked you before they bit, those fang-mouthed frosts!
So you would learn
the inward workings of your gift to men?
Zeus knew what gulfs, what peaks could teach you then
the way to burn.

.   .   .

Lie still, lie still.
It is not well for prisoners to be fed.
Shut your great eyes.
Lie still.
Oh, lullaby .   .   .
For now
they are coming, they are mounting
the terraced coast, the cliffs, climbing
the tiered clouds, filling
the blind sky
with their wings, their beaks
pointing
toward food.
It is not good
that you should see, Prometheus,
how they fly .   .   .
Your flesh
is a sweet quarry.
Though you starve, Prometheus,
they shall be richly nourished, what they snatch
shall be again renewed.
Lie still, bleed
bravely, the taloned brood
is gathered:
generations hence
it will not have ceased to feed.

[from *Prelude to Man*]

The Fourth God

CHARD POWERS SMITH

And Adam   .   .   .
.   . went from the cave and fell on the stone earth
Under the stars. .   .   .   .
.   .   .   . Then as he lay
Beaten by Man's years, like the first flare
Of life in the sea, or the first step on the land,
His will that was Man surged free from the press
Of the three gods and watched apart, seeing
The gods he was. And he knew them, and saw ahead
Their triple quest joined in one through the jungle
Of Pan's lust and Jehovah's ice walls
And the silence of Brahma's stars; until Man's will,
Aware now, should rise judge of the gods
And come to a new sun. And in self-knowledge
Of power to choose between old ways, the Fourth
God woke to his way. And Adam rose
From the earth and raised his arms. And he called strong
His challenge to new times: "The gods live
And they rule men, but Man chooses his way
Between the gods." And his long cry travelled
Eastward and westward over the hills, and its echo
Returned bringing the dawn. And the city of men
Heard in a dream, and a race stirred out of sleep
And awoke and stood amazed.
                              Then Adam moved
To the old summit over the ancient valley
And called again, "Come from this old place,
For I go into new lands." And the tribes of men,
Bearing their great spears and their stone knives,
Swarmed up from the cliffs with the huge roar
Of gigantic bees. And Adam led them northward,
And Eve with him, over the gray plains,
And westward into the hills.

· · ·

And the last man
Went from the cave where Man and his three gods
Had been formed of the hungers of two billion years.
And it yawned empty into the dead dawnlight,
The huge mouth of a frozen earth, a giant
Shell stranded, left by the tide of stars;
While from its dark chambers—the great hall
With its old niches and grots, and the outer shelter—
The memories of Man poured like the sands of the ages
Emptying back in the void. Now the years of Brahma
Poured, and Jehovan's years, and Pan's years,
Uncoiling back through the world till a man-ape roared
On a hill and Man was born. And now the coil
Spread in enormous curves back through the womb
Of time: Man fumbled with stones; he ran
On boughs; he squeaked in his den while thunder-lizards
Troubled the world; he hissed, watching his eggs;
He floated beneath ferns and his throat swelled
Piping a water song; he gasped breathing
The first spears of air. Then, like dawn reversing,
The slow green sea closed over,
And things grew dim and there was only
Light and shade and a dull and heaving sea;
The light failed; life winked in the dark;
The last coil spread to enclose the fountain
Of young stars falling back in the night
Of first Being. The Brahmin stirred. And there
Was granite in the cave where Man had been.

The red sun came from behind and curved
Over the host where Adam led westward
Up into new hills. .   .   .   .
·   ·   ·   ·   ·   ·   ·   .   And he climbed swiftly
A rock mountain and came to the last crag.
And there westward the gold sun was setting
On strange ridges piled in a jagg'd sea.

And he stood on the crag, and Eve sitting below him,
And he knew strong in his blood the great races,
The three gods, he had been, and beneath the gods
The will of Man that would mould gods to its need.
And he lifted his arms westward and knew the way
Was long ahead. And time was but thirty thousand
Years ago, and yesterday, and no more
Than the first roar of Pan, the first wheel
Of Jehovah's thought, and Brahma's first dream
Of the world's end, and the aeons unprophecied
That lie ahead along Adam's quest until
He comes to the sun and the Fourth God will be born.

. . .

　　　　　Out of the valley
The eyes of the host saw him there, a colossus
Tall on the earth's peak framed by the sun.
And a swift rumor spread through the shadowed world
Like a night gust or a fear in a strange place.
And the rumble of voices stilled, and all men
Rose from their evening work and stood silent
Gazing up into long twilight and wonder
While the great cauldron vanished behind him, tilting
Upward the mountain's shade. And still they gazed,
And not a man moved, while up from the eastward
Slowly the long shadow swung, and lifted
That form into the night, and left the stars.

You, Andrew Marvell

ARCHIBALD MACLEISH

And here face down beneath the sun
And here upon earth's noonward height
To feel the always coming on
The always rising of the night

To feel creep up the curving east
The earthy chill of dusk and slow
Upon those under lands the vast
And ever climbing shadow grow

And strange at Ecbatan the trees
Take leaf by leaf the evening strange
The flooding dark about their knees
The mountains over Persia change

And now at Kermanshah the gate
Dark empty and the withered grass
And through the twilight now the late
Few travelers in the westward pass

And Baghdad darken and the bridge
Across the silent river gone
And through Arabia the edge
Of evening widen and steal on

And deepen on Palmyra's street
The wheel rut in the ruined stone
And Lebanon fade out and Crete
High through the clouds and overblown

And over Sicily the air
Still flashing with the landward gulls
And loom and slowly disappear
The sails above the shadowy hulls

And Spain go under and the shore
Of Africa the gilded sand
And evening vanish and no more
The low pale light across that land

Nor now the long light on the sea

And here face downward in the sun
To feel how swift how secretly
The shadow of the night comes on . . .

Lines from *The Auroras of Autumn*

WALLACE STEVENS

i

This is where the serpent lives, the bodiless.
His head is air. Beneath his tip at night
Eyes open and fix on us in every sky.

•   •   •

This is form gulping after formlessness,
Skin flashing to wished-for disappearances
And the serpent body flashing without the skin.

This is the height emerging and its base
These lights may finally attain a pole
In the midmost midnight and find the serpent there,

•   •   •

ii

•   •   •

The season changes. A cold wind chills the beach.

•   •   •

The man who is walking turns blankly on the sand.
He observes how the north is always enlarging the
      change,

With its frigid brilliances, its blue-red sweeps
And gusts of great enkindlings, its polar green,
The color of ice and fire and solitude.

vi

It is a theater floating through the clouds,
Itself a cloud, although of misted rock
And mountains running like water, wave on wave,

Through waves of light. It is of cloud transformed
To cloud transformed again, idly, the way
A season changes color to no end,

Except the lavishing of itself in change,
As light changes yellow into gold and gold
To its opal elements and fire's delight,

Splashed wide-wise because it likes magnificence
And the solemn pleasures of magnificent space.
The cloud drifts idly through half-thought-of forms.

.   .   .

.   .   .   The scholar of one candle sees
An Arctic effulgence flaring on the frame
Of everything he is. And he feels afraid.

viii

.   .   .

.   .   .   these lights are not a spell of light,
A saying out of a cloud, but innocence.
An innocence of the earth.   .   .   .

.   .   .

❀ PATRIOTISM

DONALD DAVIDSON / *Lee in the Mountains*

CHARD POWERS SMITH / *New England Farmer*

JOHN GOULD FLETCHER / Lines from *Lincoln*

STEPHEN VINCENT BENÉT / Lines from *Invocation*
(from *John Brown's Body*)

HART CRANE / Lines from *Cape Hatteras*
(from *The Bridge*)

✿ *In both the neo-romantic and the semi-classical schools, the* emotion called patriotism was looked at askance. Both schools reckoned it among the mob or "servile" emotions, and held it one of the psychological causes of evil in the world. Nevertheless it is an emotion which stirred a few excellent poets of the '20's not given to hysteria, and produced at least four passages of great poetry.

Donald Davidson's celebration of the Old South has the combined power and tenderness of that great aristocracy which will yet make its contribution to the reborn nation of the future.

My piece on New England is included because I wanted some recognition of New England as one of our two ancient cultures to which many people are still devoted. I couldn't find any other celebration of it written during or near the twenties, because that was the high period of the absurd debunking of everything related to the Puritans!

John Gould Fletcher was one of the Imagists-Vers Librists of the twenties. Paradoxically, although one of their professions was verbal economy and the *mot juste*, Fletcher is one of the near great poets of the twenties who almost buried his poetic greatness in contrived analogies and other verbiage. I am confident that I have improved his magnificent piece on *Lincoln* by cutting it approximately in half.

Stephen Vincent Benét's *John Brown's Body* expands patriotism from the two great sections of the nation to the nation as a whole. As an account of the conflict of issues, human and social, of the Confederate War, it has never seemed to me that the poem fulfilled its enormous intention. Yet there are in it several passages of the highest lyrical excellence, and among these, at least the *Invocation* has the sweep of greatness. The patriotism here is of the traditional sort, the emotion objective in that it is projected into identification with the land and the nation, but subjective in that it is the poet's self that is thus projected. Stephen Benét was sympathetic to both of the cultures, the sub-nations, with which he had to deal, his identification with the South being somewhat stronger than that with the North. But his dominating passion was for the inclusive geographic panorama in its magnitude, and for the epic of the Westward Movement, rather than for those of either Southern chivalry or Northern idealism. Benét's poetry is often dismissed by the critics because of its popular, its Kiplingesque, flavor. It seems to me that the criterion is simply whether it is poetry, whether it conveys to the imagination, rather than to the fancy or to the simple recognition, an emotionalized percept. And in this context there is the further question of whether the percept has the size essential to the sense of greatness. Surely the answer to both questions with respect to *Invocation*, is affirmative.

Hart Crane's devotion to America proclaims itself almost everywhere throughout *The Bridge*. Being inspired by Whitman, and its expression often derived from him, it is of the order of a passionate, personal love, and has none of the aggressive, often military, quality that is usually associated with patriotism.

Lee in the Mountains 1865–1870

DONALD DAVIDSON

Walking into the shadows, walking alone
Where the sun falls through the ruined boughs of locusts
Up to the president's office.   .   .   .
                               Hearing the voices
Whisper, *Hush, it is General Lee!* And strangely
Hearing my own voice say, *Good morning, boys.*
(*Don't get up. You are early. It is long*
before the bell. You will have long to wait
on these cold steps. . . .)
                          The young have time to wait.
But soldiers' faces under their tossing flags
Lift no more by any road or field,
And I am spent with old wars and new sorrow.
Walking the rocky path, where steps decay
And the paint cracks and grass eats on the stone.
It is not General Lee, young men   .   .   .
It is Robert Lee in a dark civilian suit who walks,
An outlaw fumbling for the latch, a voice
Commanding in a dream where no flag flies.

My father's house is taken and his hearth
Left to the candle-drippings where the ashes
Whirl at a chimney-breath on the cold stone.
I can hardly remember my father's look, I cannot
Answer his voice as he calls farewell in the misty
Mounting where riders gather at gates.
He was old then—I was a child—his hand
Held out for mine, some daybreak snatched away,
And he rode out, a broken man. Now let
His lone grave keep, surer than cypress roots,
The vow I made beside him. God too late
Unseals to certain eyes the drift
Of time and the hopes of men and a sacred cause.
The fortune of the Lees goes with the land
Whose sons will keep it still. My mother
Told me much. She sat among the candles,
Fingering the *Memoirs*, now so long unread.
And as my pen moves on across the page
Her voice comes back, a murmuring distillation
Of old Virginia times now faint and gone,
The hurt of all that was and cannot be.

Why did my father write? I know he saw
History clutched as a wraith out of blowing mist
Where tongues are loud, and a glut of little souls
Laps at the too much blood and the burning house.
He would have his say, but I shall not have mine.
What I do is only a son's devoir
To a lost father. Let him only speak.
The rest must pass to men who never knew
(But on a written page) the strike of armies,
And never heard the long Confederate cry
Charge through the muzzling smoke or saw the bright
Eyes of the beardless boys go up to death.
It is Robert Lee who writes with his father's hand—
The rest must go unsaid and the lips be locked.

If all were told, as it cannot be told—
If all the dread opinion of the heart

Now could speak, now in the shame and torment
Lashing the bound and trampled States—

If a word were said, as it cannot be said—

I see clear waters run in Virginia's valley
And in the house the weeping of young women
Rises no more. The waves of grain begin.
The Shenandoah is golden with new grain.
The Blue Ridge, crowned with a haze of light,
Thunders no more. The horse is at plough. The rifle
Returns to the chimney crotch and the hunter's hand.
And nothing else than this? Was it for this
That on an April day we stacked our arms
Obedient to a soldier's trust? To lie
Ground by heels of little men,
Forever maimed, defeated, lost, impugned?
And was I then betrayed? Did I betray?

If it were said, as still it might be said—
If it were said, and a word should run like fire,
Like living fire into the roots of grass,
The sunken flag would kindle on wild hills,
The brooding hearts would waken, and the dream
Stir like a crippled phantom under the pines,
And this torn earth would quicken into shouting
Beneath the feet of ragged bands—
                                    The pen
Turns to the waiting page, the sword
Bows to the rust that cankers and the silence.

Among these boys whose eyes lift up to mine
Within gray walls where droning wasps repeat
A hollow reveillé, I still must face,
Day after day, the courier with his summons
Once more to surrender, now to surrender all.
Without arms or men I stand, but with knowledge only
I face what long I saw, before others knew,

When Pickett's men streamed back, and I heard the tangled
Cry of the Wilderness wounded, bloody with doom.

The mountains, once I said, in the little room
At Richmond, by the huddled fire, but still
The President shook his head. The mountains wait,
I said, in the long beat and rattle of siege
At cratered Petersburg. Too late
We sought the mountains and those people came.
And Lee is in mountains now, beyond Appomattox,
Listening long for voices that never will speak
Again; hearing the hoofbeats come and go and fade
Without a stop, without a brown hand lifting
The tent-flap, or a bugle call at dawn,
Or ever on the long white road the flag
Of Jackson's quick brigades. I am alone,
Trapped, consenting, taken at last in mountains.

It is not the bugle now, or the long roll beating.
The simple stroke of a chapel bell forbids
The hurtling dream, recalls the lonely mind.
Young men, the God of your fathers is a just
And merciful God Who in this blood once shed
On your green altars measures out all days,
And measures out the grace
Whereby alone we live;
And in His might He waits,
Brooding within the certitude of time,
To bring this lost forsaken valor
And the fierce faith undying
And the love quenchless
To flower among the hills to which we cleave,
To fruit upon the mountains whither we flee,
Never forsaking, never denying
His children and His children's children forever
Unto all generations of the faithful heart.

New England Farmer

CHARD POWERS SMITH

They stood once in this new land
Where the snow roamed and the cold came.
To the stone hills they gave a name,
Where our fathers stood once, we stand.

They stood young when the red sun
Was a grael glow on the western line,
And the wind flowed in the black pine
With a peace promise for work done.

They stood with a strong god and a known
Faith's way to a soul's place,
And the church bell at the hill's base
Was a clanged laugh at the cold's moan.

And leaves budded and leaves blew
In the fall wind. And they walled stones.
And they bred the earth with their sires' bones,
And the earth quickened and wealth grew.

The thing is done: The wealth fails;
The god dies; and the red sun
Is a dead mock of the thing done;
The cold returns, and the white gales.

We are nothing now but the known men
With the known hills and the known streams—
What a man is when his blown dreams
Settle to seed in the soil again.

We are nothing here in this old land
But the soul bred in its grey earth
Out of rock strength and of time's mirth.
Where our fathers stood once, we stand.

Lines from *Lincoln*

JOHN GOULD FLETCHER

i

Like a gaunt, scraggly pine
Which lifts its head above the mournful sandhills;
And patiently, through dull years of bitter silence,
Untended and uncared for, starts to grow.

Ungainly, laboring, huge,
The wind of the north has twisted and gnarled its branches;
Yet in the heat of mid-summer days, when thunder clouds
    ring the horizon,
A nation of men shall rest beneath its shade.

• • •

iii

There is a silence abroad in the land to-day,
And in the hearts of men, a deep and anxious silence;
And, because we are still at last, those bronze lips slowly
    open,
Those hollow and weary eyes take on a gleam of light.

Slowly a patient, firm-syllabled voice cuts through the
    endless silence,
Like laboring oxen that drag a plough through the chaos
    of rude clay-fields,
"I went forward as the light goes forward in early spring,
But there were also many things which I left behind.

• • •

"Have you forgotten your graves? Go, question them in
    anguish,
Listen long to their unstirred lips. From your hostages to
    silence
Learn there is no life without death, no dawn without sun-
    setting,
No victory but to him who has given all."

The clamor of cannon dies down, the furnace-mouth of the
    battle is silent,
The midwinter sun dips and descends, the earth takes on
    afresh its bright colors.
But he whom we mocked and obeyed not, he whom we
    scorned and mistrusted,
He has descended, like a god, to his rest.

Over the uproar of cities,
Over the million intricate threads of life wavering and cross-
    ing
In the midst of problems we know not, tangling, perplexing,
    ensnaring,
Rises one white tomb alone.

Beam over it, stars,
Wrap it 'round, stripes—stripes red for the pain that he bore for
    you—
Enfold it forever, O flag, rent, soiled, but repaired through
    your anguish;
Long as you keep him there safe, the nations shall bow to
    your law.

Strew over him flowers:
Blue forget-me-nots from the north and the bright pink
    arbutus
From the east, and from the west rich orange blossom,
But from the heart of the land take the passion-flower;
Rayed, violet, dim,
With the nails that pierced, the cross that he bore and the
    circlet,
And beside it there lay also one lonely snow-white magnolia,
Bitter for remembrance of the healing which has passed.

[from *John Brown's Body*]

Lines from *Invocation*

STEPHEN VINCENT BENÉT

American muse, whose strong and diverse heart
So many men have tried to understand
But only made it smaller with their art,
Because you are as various as your land,

As mountainous-deep, as flowered with blue rivers,
Thirsty with deserts, buried under snows,
As native as the shape of Navajo quivers,
And native, too, as the sea-voyaged rose.

Swift runner, never captured or subdued,
Seven-branched elk beside the mountain stream,
That half a hundred hunters have pursued
But never matched their bullets with the dream,

Where the great huntsmen failed, I set my sorry
And mortal snare for your immortal quarry.

You are the buffalo-ghost, the broncho-ghost
With dollar-silver in your saddle-horn,
The cowboys riding in from Painted Post,
The Indian arrow in the Indian corn,

And you are the clipped velvet of the lawns
Where Shropshire grows from Massachusetts sods,
The grey Maine rocks—and the war-painted dawns
That break above the Garden of the Gods.

The prairie-schooners crawling toward the ore
And the cheap car, parked by the station-door.

Where the skyscrapers lift their foggy plumes
Of stranded smoke out of a stony mouth

You are that high stone and its arrogant fumes,
And you are ruined gardens in the South

And bleak New England farms, so winter-white
Even their roofs look lonely, and the deep
The middle grainland where the wind of night
Is like all blind earth sighing in her sleep.

A friend, an enemy, a sacred hag
With two tied oceans in her medicine-bag.

They tried to fit you with an English song
And clip your speech into the English tale.
But, even from the first, the words went wrong,
The catbird pecked away the nightingale.

The homesick men begot high-cheekboned things
Whose wit was whittled with a different sound
And Thames and all the rivers of the kings
Ran into Mississippi and were drowned.

.   .   .

I think that I have seen you, not as one,
But clad in diverse semblances and powers,
Always the same, as light falls from the sun,
And always different, as the differing hours.

Yet, through each altered garment that you wore,
The naked body, shaking the heart's core.

All day the snow fell on that Eastern town
With its soft, pelting, little, endless sigh
Of infinite flakes that brought the tall sky down
Till I could put my hands in the white sky

And taste cold scraps of heaven on my tongue
And walk in such a changed and luminous light

As Gods inhabit when the Gods are young.
All day it fell. And when the gathered night

Was a blue shadow cast by a pale glow
I saw you then, snow-image, bird of the snow.

And I have seen and heard you in the dry
Close-huddled furnace of the city street
When the parched moon was planted in the sky
And the limp air hung dead against the heat.

I saw you rise, red as that rusty plant,
Dizzied with lights, half-mad with senseless sound,
Enormous metal, shaking to the chant
Of a triphammer striking iron ground.

Enormous power, ugly to the fool,
And beautiful as a well-handled tool.

These, and the memory of that windy day
On the bare hills, beyond the last barbed wire,
When all the orange poppies bloomed one way
As if a breath would blow them into fire,

I keep forever, like the sea-lion's tusk
The broken sailor brings away to land,
But when he touches it, he smells the musk,
And the whole sea lies hollow in his hand.

So, from a hundred visions, I make one,
And out of darkness build my mocking sun.

[from *The Bridge*]

Lines from *Cape Hatteras*

HART CRANE

                    Thou, there beyond—
Glacial sierras and the flight of ravens,
Hermetically past condor zones, through zenith havens
Past where the albatross has offered up
His last wing-pulse, and downcast as a cup
That's drained, is shivered back to earth—thy wand
Has beat a song, O Walt,—there and beyond!
And this, thine other hand, upon my heart
Is plummet ushered of those tears that start
What memories of vigils, bloody, by that Cape,—
Ghoul-mound of man's perversity at balk
And fraternal massacre! Thou, pallid there as chalk,
Hast kept of wounds, O Mourner, all that sum
That then from Appomattox stretched to Somme!

Cowslip and shad-blow, flaked like tethered foam
Around bared teeth of stallions, bloomed that spring
When first I read thy lines, rife as the loam
Of prairies, yet like breakers cliffward leaping!
O, early following thee, I searched the hill
Blue-writ and odor-firm with violets, 'til
With June the mountain laurel broke through green
And filled the forest with what clustrous sheen!
Potomac lilies,—then the Pontiac rose,
And Klondike edelweiss of occult snows!
White banks of moonlight came descending valleys—
How speechful on oak-vizored palisades,
As vibrantly I following down Sequoia alleys
Heard thunder's eloquence through green arcades
Set trumpets breathing in each clump and grass tuft—'til
Gold autumn, captured, crowned the trembling hill!

Panis Angelicus! Eyes tranquil with the blaze
Of love's own diametric gaze, of love's amaze!
Not greatest, thou,—not first, nor last,—but near
And onward yielding past my utmost year.
Familiar, thou, as mendicants in public places;
Evasive—too—as dayspring's spreading arc to trace
    is:—
Our Meistersinger, thou set breath in steel;
And it was thou who on the boldest heel
Stood up and flung the span on even wing
Of that great Bridge, our Myth, whereof I sing!

❀ THE HUMAN CONDITION

WILLIAM CARLOS WILLIAMS / *The Yachts*

ARCHIBALD MACLEISH / *Epistle to Be Left in the Earth*

HORACE GREGORY / Lines from *Chorus for Survival*

WALLACE STEVENS / Lines from *Sunday Morning* / Lines
from *On the Road Home* / Lines from *It Must Be
Abstract* (from *Notes Toward A Supreme Fiction*) /
Lines from *It Must Change* (From *Notes Toward A
Supreme Fiction*)

MARIANNE MOORE / *In Distrust of Merits*

JAMES RORTY / Lines from *Avenger, What Wrong?*

HART CRANE / Lines from *Cape Hatteras* (from *The Bridge*)

ANNA HEMPSTEAD BRANCH / Lines from *The Descendant
and the Id*

GEORGE SANTAYANA / *Sonnets vii and xxv*

LÉONIE ADAMS / *Thought's End*

WINIFRED WELLES / *Cruciform*

ROBERT FROST / *Bereft* / *West-Running Brook*

EDWIN ARLINGTON ROBINSON / *Mr. Flood's Party* /
Karma / From *Octaves* / *Two Sonnets, ii*

❀ *These are the poets' comments on life as a whole, together with* their solutions except in so far as the latter are presented elsewhere. Without exception the spectacle presented of man on the earth is a sombre one, but with two exceptions each of these thirteen poets attains, here or elsewhere in this book, some affirmative solution, such as the members of the Lost Generation felt instinctively was to be found.

Only Williams and MacLeish leave us with negation uncompensated. Williams was exceptional in the twenties, being a kind of roughneck classicist chiefly concerned with brutal, material reality unalleviated, so far as I know, by any search for either humanist or transcendental truth. MacLeish stands as the literary tragedy of the period, for he writes with strong romantic motility, yet seems unable to attain and retain the substantial affirmation intimated by his style, let alone any settled classical conclusion. *Epistle to be Left in the Earth* is a statement of unrelieved disillusion with humanity and its prospects, beautifully portrayed on a cosmic canvas which gives it the sweep of greatness. Yet in view of a thinness in the style, and considering the whole output of this highly talented poet, it is impossible to say whether the poem expresses a profoundly felt negative perception or whether it is merely another brilliant adaptation to the period. Equipped with extreme verbal fluency, facility in poetic expression, a richly stored and disciplined mind, and general versatility which has carried him with initial success into almost every category of experience, MacLeish has yet advanced little beyond the confusion of his early *Hamlet*, and one wonders whether all of his output is more than a kaleidoscopic outpouring of brilliant fancy. He has swung with the major turns of politics and literary fashion, has been adroit enough to jump early into the leadership of some. Yet these changes have not represented growth, and finally he remains where he started. MacLeish does not even swing all the way to the shambles that Williams honestly revels in. Apparently not persuaded by the ultimate self-loss of Job, no more did he, in *J.B.*, enlarge upon human ego-centricity; instead, he must garble the great story of proto-Christianity with much unoriginal, self-assertive bombast. The selection in this section is, so far as I know, the greatest surrender of a fine mind in the American record.

In attempting to compile the major statements about life by poets of the twenties, it is a relief to turn from the negation of Williams and the incomplete romanticism of MacLeish to the clear, unpretentious humanist affirmations of the classicists Gregory and Stevens. The passage from *Chorus For Survival* is a great hymn to love as the solution of life in a predatory age, a crusading affirmation of it all the way from childhood memories to mature domesticity and social concern. (It is because of the predominance of the latter that the poem is included here instead of in the section on Love.) Although Gregory's poem is deeply felt and dramatized, and is not much reasoned in expression, it is in essence a humanist affirmation of Christian truth without benefit of emotionalized mystical perception, an early statement of the direction some of the theologians are taking toward "Christianity without Religion."

As distinguished from his co-classicist Gregory, Stevens was a purely intellectual poet, both in analysis and in expression, the only one, so far as I know, who managed to emerge in the generally anti-intellectual atmosphere of the twenties. Rather than an exemplar of that period, he was a prophet of the forties. He professed none of the doctrines that were fashionable at the time of publication of his first book in 1923. His supreme self-preoccupation had nothing to do with self-expression. His interest in sex, like his greater interest in beauty, was philosophical only. He was neither simple, sensuous, nor passionate. By the dominant literary standard of the twenties, as distinguished from those of the *avant garde* that was going to be the New Criticism, he was not a poet at all. His early technical craftsmanship was indifferent, his phonetic quality being provided by the absurd jingling and jangling of his "blue guitar." He showed, and continued to show throughout his life, a shocking ignorance of nature and its wealth of imagery for tropeic use; his metaphors for external objects, when he attempted them, were usually inept, unpoetic, the work either of careless fancy or of unsuccessful contrivance. He shared none of the romanticism of the twenties, being intellectual rather than emotional, static rather than motile, objective rather than subjective, even in his observation of himself. Through this, his early period, and decreasingly thereafter, he was guilty of the compulsion to astound with exotic words—not to mention coined ones—which characterized the followers of Pound and the

New Criticism; but at the end of his life he added solid clarity to his other classical qualities.

Yet for all his disqualifications by romantic standards, he was a poet indeed, and a great one, perhaps not the greatest but at least the most independent and original of his generation. In an age that abhorred "glittering generalities," he used them continuously. Surrounded by critics who condemned philosophical, or otherwise intellectual, inquiry as fatal to poetry, he indulged in almost nothing else. For him real experience was not a function of the body and its emotions, but of the mind. His lifelong subject was the activity of his own mind, within its enclosing metaphysical world, without concern for the physical phantasmagoria, including the brain, that hung between them, whether as curtain or conductor. And in his reporting of that activity he wrote genuine poetry consistently, using precise and often magnificent figures for inner experience. He was not a mystic. To the best of my observation he was not an absolutist of any kind; or perhaps more accurately, he recognized the probable existence of absolute reality, but within his humanist, classical arena he must not affirm what was supernatural. The one thing he shared with his generation was the quest for truth, in his case rational, in a spiritual void. Whether or not he arrived at any conclusion which might stand as a philosophical contribution, he did make his search for it in great poetry. His real world is the quietly shining one of thought, the colors cool in light blues and greens, with no more gold than the sometimes glitter of it, no more red than is subdued in lavender, and before all colors a kaleidoscope of mist always turning, like his northern lights in *The Auroras of Autumn*. This is the world in which we all live consciously or unconsciously, but Stevens is the only poet in English literature who not only lived in it consciously all the time but devoted all of his imaginative energy to its portrayal.

Throughout his life Stevens improved in prosody, especially in euphony and in cadence—always some easy variation upon his traditional instinct for pentameter or tetrameter. *Sunday Morning*, the first poem quoted here, shows his state of development in the early twenties—indifferent technique, mild sensuousness, especially visual, gentle cynicism, gentle hedonism, incipient relativism and pluralism. In *On the Road Home*, probably written in the thirties, the technique is sure and the anti-absolutist tendencies have matured and find expression in a rare juxtaposition of philosophical statement and natural symbols. In *Notes Toward A Supreme Fiction*, written in the forties, and from which I have offered other excerpts in other sections of this book, we have the mature mind telling us particular truth after truth that it has learned, each revelation less than ultimate. I feel less compunction about excerpting Stevens than most of the other poets I have violated in this fashion. Not that he overwrites. Rather, in his mature style, each section of his long poems is a complete work of art, and within it each detail, each brush stroke, at once makes its contribution to the whole and is complete in itself and worth noting for its own sake. And what I say here, to justify my dissection of the text, is one of the things Stevens tells us about the arts of the human and cosmic processes.

With justification on several grounds Marianne Moore was claimed by the semi-classicists of the New Criticism. But ultimately she is no classicist, because of her final necessity, illustrated in *What Are Years?*, already given, to make some kind of transcendental affirmation. *In Distrust of Merits* is one of the most inclusive of those poems of hers, mentioned earlier, which have the sweep of greatness but are implemented mostly in prosaic uses both of language and of rhythm. Here there is more poetry in detail than is usual in these poems of weighty substance; the recurrent refrain almost provides a prosodic backbone; and the imaginative overtone is as large as the whole human condition. In scope this poem is coextensive with Gregory's as a statement of "Christianity without Religion." Miss Moore declares the necessity of self-loss, and Gregory affirms the love that makes the self-loss possible.

Rorty's *Avenger, What Wrong?* returns, in mostly rhetorical verse, to the brutality of Williams's world, but with the difference of an incredulity that leaves room for affirmation beyond the tremendous figure of the sub-humanity into which we are hurrying. Crane's portrayal of the machine age is less overwhelming, less great, and more poetic than Rorty's. And the spectacle is still offset by the Whitman-like, affirmative compulsion that was illustrated earlier. In connection with both Rorty's and Crane's condemnation of the technological world, a reference might be made to Hildegarde Flanner's celebration of the cosmic grace of the machine, in the section on "Beauty."

Anna Hempstead Branch, like Conrad Aiken, did not entirely escape from the basic weakness of Victorian poetry. Emotionalized, imaginative perception must needs be elaborated by "thoughts," and the text accordingly padded with eloquent, versified prose. Stripped of its padding, the central structure of *The Descendant and the Id*, presented here, stands as a very great poem, setting out the hopeless impotence imposed on modern man by the doctrine of biological determinism. The hopelessness continues without relief until the end, when suddenly the despair is swept away in a surge of genuine, proto-mystical perception of essential Being, duly celebrated by a flourish of romantic self-assertion.

In this section I have presented two of Santayana's sonnets, published in 1906, including them because, in spite of his Roman Catholic classicism, he addressed life with a materialistic and romantically hopeful despair which foreshadowed the twenties, and because these sonnets were respected by the poets of that period. In fulfilment of his romantic aspiration, compare his sonnet of unorthodox Mystical Realization which appears in the final section of this book.

Léonie Adams's *Thought's End* is given here because of the last line, one of those statements of a simple poetic greatness which it would seem that anyone with talent might have written, only, mysteriously, nobody but Miss Adams did.

Winifred Welles, an unjustly neglected New England poet of mystical perception and delicacy of expression reminiscent of Emily Dickinson, finds some compensation for the hopeless earthly state, proclaimed here, in highly original intimations of immortality presented in the next section.

Frost's comments on life are mostly partial and inferential in his dramatic pieces, with a few more inclusive romantic and mystical affirmations. *Bereft* is a pessimistic statement of loneliness, and *West-Running Brook* is a humanist partial affirmation: each of us can make one little splash, one little fillip of independent personality, even while the main stream of our years runs off into oblivion. Several times, as in the last section of this book, Frost professes Mystical Realization. But it is not complete enough to replace his homely humanism as the continuing aura of his poetry.

There is probably no poem of Robinson's, whether dramatic or lyric, that is not an intentional comment on life. In order to amass the total comment it would be necessary to read with some care the largest bulk of verse published by an American, being—at a rough count—fifty-one dramatic sonnets, eighty-four other dramatic poems, twenty-eight contemplative sonnets, twenty-eight other contemplative poems, and twelve epics, the entire array involving 288 characters developed at least in some essential quality—the largest population of any poet in English except those who wrote for the stage. A reasonably thorough sampling might be had from the four epics *Merlin, Lancelot, The Man Who Died Twice*, and *Matthias at the Door*, and the micro-epic *The Three Taverns!*

In order to keep within moderate bounds, the offering of Robinson's comment on the Human Condition is here limited to four poems, including one short drama, *Mr. Flood's Party*, one character sonnet, *Karma*, and eighteen of the twenty-three little read *Octaves* which, reflecting the first major crisis in Robinson's life, express perhaps the largest quantum of poetically implemented wisdom that can be found in so few pages anywhere. The second of the contemplative *Two Sonnets*, prescribing thought as the method of inviting Mystical Realization, is transitional to the later section of that title. Most of Robinson's contemplative poems, and many of the dramatic ones, contain mystical facets, as most of his mystical poems contain implications regarding the immediate Human Condition. The partition of poems between the two sections, therefore, is more or less arbitrary, depending on a difference in emphasis rather than on the exclusive identification of any poem with either of the topics.

WILLIAM CARLOS WILLIAMS
The Yachts

contend in a sea which the land partly encloses
shielding them from the too-heavy blows
of an ungoverned ocean which when it chooses

tortures the biggest hulls, the best man knows
to pit against its beatings, and sinks them pitilessly.
Mothlike in mists, scintillant in the minute

brilliance of cloudless days, with broad bellying sails
they glide to the wind tossing green water
from their sharp prows while over them the crew crawls

ant-like, solicitously grooming them, releasing,
making fast as they turn, lean far over and having
caught the wind again, side by side, head for the mark.

In a well guarded arena of open water surrounded by
lesser and greater craft which, sycophant, lumbering
and flittering follow them, they appear youthful, rare

as the light of a happy eye, live with the grace
of all that in the mind is feckless, free and
naturally to be desired. Now the sea which holds them

is moody, lapping their glossy sides, as if feeling
for some slightest flaw but fails completely.
Today no race. Then the wind comes again. The yachts

move, jockeying for a start, the signal is set and they
are off. Now the waves strike at them but they are too
well made, they slip through, though they take in canvas.

Arms with hands grasping seek to clutch at the prows.
Bodies thrown recklessly in the way are cut aside.
It is a sea of faces about them in agony, in despair

until the horror of the race dawns staggering the mind,
the whole sea become an entanglement of watery bodies
lost to the world bearing what they cannot hold. Broken,

beaten, desolate, reaching from the dead to be taken up
they cry out, failing, failing! their cries rising
in waves still as the skillful yachts pass over.

Epistle to be Left in the Earth

ARCHIBALD MACLEISH

. . . It is colder now
                        there are many stars
                                      we are drifting
North by the Great Bear
                    the leaves are falling
The water is stone in the scooped rocks
                              to southward
Red sun grey air
             the crows are
Slow on their crooked wings
                        the jays have left us
Long since we passed the flares of Orion
Each man believes in his heart he will die
Many have written last thoughts and last letters
None know if our deaths are now or forever
None know if this wandering earth will be found

We lie down and snow covers our garments
I pray you
            you (if any open this writing)
Make in your mouths the words that were our names
I will tell you all we have learned
                        I will tell you everything
The earth is round
               there are springs under the orchards
The loam cuts with a blunt knife
                    beware of
Elms in thunder
              the lights in the sky are stars
We think they do not see
                   we think also
The trees do not know nor the leaves of the grasses
                            hear us

The birds too are ignorant
                        Do not listen
Do not stand at dark in the open windows
We before you have heard this
                          they are voices
They are not words at all but the wind rising
Also none among us has seen God
(. . . We have thought often
The flaws of sun in the late and driving weather
Pointed to one tree but it was not so)
As for the nights I warn you the nights are dangerous
The wind changes at night and the dreams come

It is very cold
                    there are strange stars near Arcturus

Voices are crying an unknown name in the sky

[From *Collected Poems*]

Lines from *Chorus for Survival*

HORACE GREGORY

i

Tell us that love
               returns,
O Hymen, sing
In every hour that burns
After the midnight hour
In darkness here.
                 Wake with thy song
The antique smiling year,
Always thy axis turning to restore
The Greek dawn breaking
On Aegean seas.

. . .

Wake with thy song
                    time-darkened waters
That have not reached their end
Westward to India, passage through storm,
Bearing the image of a Grecian bride,
Eyes like cornflowers staring at our side,
The blue flame lighting darkness in the shade
Of trees knee-deep in grass
At summer's tide. . . .
Again our lips recall
That she was beautiful:
                        the pure
Alcestis memory of a kiss,
                        the violet-
Scented breast, the virginal
Breathing light in sunlit air;
Handclasp remembers hand,
                          quick limbs enthrall
Entwining limbs, the nervous, flexible,
Growing green grapevine,
                        until the blood
Flows into sleep and blood is wine.

This is thy memory, America,
The tenuous marriage of disunited blood,
Captain and slave one bed,
                          in dust until the wind
Stirs dust to life again . . .
                          and walking here,
Conquered and conqueror
(The apple blossoms white in midnight hair).

Wake with thy song
Even in death (they sleep like death)
Men in the wilderness

(The night is long)
              breaking through forests of a foreign land,
Sell and move on.
Westward we follow to an unknown star
And shall not come again the way we came.

Tell us that love
           returns
After the midnight hour
In darkness here,

Season of iron cities against the sky,
The cold room where I write my signature
Toward my survival in the waning year:
Winter and frost, each day revolves to night,
The longer night that brings a short tomorrow
Of middle age in dark, divided faces,
In faces that I know too well, my own
Face staring likeness in the mirror
Beyond the hour of death or hope or doom;
When doors swing wide upon an empty room,
Window and door open to empty air
Echo in darkness of the lost frontier.

Wake with thy song
              the voices
Of men who cannot sleep:
                  We count our losses
In decimals of time, the ten per cent
Of what we hope: To let:
                   the naked bed, the folding chair,
Space for the body motionless in air,
Permit survival if we stand alone.
Voiceless we smile; we are not violent.

And from these places
On the abyss of loss,
              the steel-edged towers

Pierce the moon, the sun:
Look where Atlantis leaves forgotten traces,
Empire of empty houses under seas.

This is thy heritage, America,
Scaffold of iron deep in stone.
                              Destroy the ruins,
This is the place; wreck here and build again.

Tell us that love
                    returns,
Not soft nor kind,
But like a crystal turning in the mind,
Light where the body is:
                              thy limbs are fire
Walking alive among the ancient trees,
The ruined town, cathedral wall, church spire.

Say love, though always young,
Remembers these . . .
                        place, house we entered
And shall not return . . .
                              Spirit that outlives time
To join our hands in love,
                          do you remember
Serpent and dove, the wild rose and the thorn,
Blossom and leaf in secret flowering
Read in a book of broken prophecies?

•   •   •

                          [From *Poems 1930-1940*]

iii
Poet and friend, how many times have I
Wished to forget your image at the door,
told you:
            Get out before we starve,
before the house rots and my days are gone,
the more we talk, the more we're undone.

"Loaf and invite the soul," the deer that strays
into my hands, the silver beast
with children's eyes, feed it once more;
count this day lost, say all my years are emptied,
a paragraph in old newspaper files:
My arms embracing hero, heroine,
whose love, whose death; whose race won and whose cheers?
All set in type and each bright face forgotten.

We have been poor together,
hating each other,
breaking our hopes, our lives,
and known that terror waits at each street corner:
gain, loss, sweepstake or ruin at day's end.
Exit before we sleep—not death, but living
with no name,
the mind gone and the smile returning, *Yes.*
Where did I put my hat? Always the same.

Meet X, the scientist, exploding ions
in basement quiet, sane: measures electron
B, the steady hand arrives at no decision:
"Wait! for the day's too short, and night's too long;
wait for the square root of the heart of X
in physics, metaphysics, Einstein, Marx,
somewhere the calibration is concealed,
the perfect temperature, until the glass
breaks, I begin . . ."
X, tired, relaxed, does not commit himself
(even to death) "See how I wake each morning
to hope (it is not easy) to survive."

Hear Y, the Communist at Union Square,
Lenin's great hand against the sky, the lips declaiming:
"Down, metaphysics down; up heart, up fire
To burn old doubt and fear.
                              Pay as you enter to the house of gold
and through this door glide parasite millionaire,

poet and engineer: check body, soul
with overcoat and stick,
the delicate laboratory brains of men
are all subzero here."

.   .   .

And each man separates,
as you and I break handclasp, turn
remembering unpaid debts, unanswered letters,
the lighted clock above an empty square
waits for the hour to strike,
       strike Monday morning,
"They gave me murder when I asked for bread,
now, guns and battleships."
      Yes and goodnight,
they shall not find me dead,
       turn with me as I go
between the fire and the bright winter's cold.

         [from *Collected Poems*]

iv
Ask no return for love that's given
embracing mistress, wife or friend,
       ask no return:
on this deep earth or in pale heaven,
awake and spend
hands, lips, and eyes in love,
in darkness burn,
    the limbs entwined until the soul ascend.

Ask no return of seasons gone:
the fire of autumn and the first hour of spring,
the short bough blossoming
through city windows when night's done,
when fears adjourn
    backward in memory where all loves end

in self again, again the inward tree
growing against the heart
and no heart free.
From love that sleeps behind each eye
in double symmetry
                              ask no return,
even in enmity, look! I shall take your hand;
nor can our limbs disjoin in separate ways again,
walking, even at night on foreign land
through houses open to the wind, through cold and rain,
waking alive, meet, kiss, and understand.

Lines from *Sunday Morning*

WALLACE STEVENS

i

Complacencies of the peignoir, and late
Coffee and oranges in a sunny chair,
And the green freedom of a cockatoo
Upon a rug mingle to dissipate
The holy hush of ancient sacrifice.
She dreams a little, and she feels the dark
Encroachment of that old catastrophe,

.   .   .

The day is like wide water, without sound,
Stilled for the passing of her dreaming feet
Over the seas, to silent Palestine,
Dominion of the blood and sepulchre.

ii

Why should she give her bounty to the dead?
What is divinity if it can come
Only in silent shadows and in dreams?

Shall she not find in comforts of the sun,
In pungent fruit and bright green wings, or else
In any balm or beauty of the earth,
Things to be cherished like the thought of heaven?
Divinity must live within herself:
Passions of rain, or moods in falling snow;
Grievings in loneliness, or unsubdued
Elations when the forest blooms; gusty
Emotions on wet roads on autumn nights;
All pleasures and all pains, remembering
The bough of summer and the winter branch.
These are the measures destined for her soul.

v

She says, "But in contentment I still feel
The need of some imperishable bliss."
Death is the mother of beauty; hence from her
Alone, shall come fulfilment to our dreams
And our desires. Although she strews the leaves
Of sure obliteration on our paths,
The path sick sorrow took, the many paths
Where triumph rang its brassy phrase, or love
Whispered a little out of tenderness,

.   .   .

vi

Is there no change of death in paradise?
Does ripe fruit never fall? Or do the boughs
Hang always heavy in that perfect sky,
Unchanging, yet so like our perishing earth,
With rivers like our own that seek for seas
They never find, the same receding shores
That never touch with inarticulate pang?

.   .   .

Death is the mother of beauty, mystical,
Within whose burning bosom we devise
Our earthly mothers waiting, sleeplessly.

viii

She hears, upon that water without sound,
A voice that cries, "The tomb in Palestine
Is not the porch of spirits lingering.
It is the grave of Jesus, where he lay."
We live in an old chaos of the sun,
Or old dependency of day and night,
Or island solitude, unsponsored, free,
Of that wide water, inescapable.
Deer walk upon our mountains, and the quail
Whistle about us their spontaneous cries;
Sweet berries ripen in the wilderness;
And, in the isolation of the sky,
At evening, casual flocks of pigeons make
Ambiguous undulations as they sink,
Downward to darkness, on extended wings.

Lines from *On the Road Home*

WALLACE STEVENS

It was when I said,
"There is no such thing as the truth,"
That the grapes seemed fatter.
The fox ran out of his hole.

You . . . You said,
"There are many truths,
But they are not parts of a truth."
Then the tree, at night, began to change,

Smoking through green and smoking blue.
We were two figures in a wood.
We said we stood alone.

It was when I said,
"Words are not forms of a single word.
In the sum of the parts, there are only the parts.
The world must be measured by eye";

. . .

It was at that time, that the silence was largest
And longest, the night was roundest,
The fragrance of the autumn warmest,
Closest and strongest.

[from *Notes Toward
A Supreme Fiction*]

Lines from *It Must Be Abstract*

WALLACE STEVENS

vii

. . .

                        . . . Perhaps
The truth depends on a walk around a lake,

A composing as the body tires, a stop
To see hepatica, a stop to watch
A definition growing certain and

A wait within that certainty, a rest
In the swags of pine-trees bordering the lake.
Perhaps there are times of inherent excellence,

As when the cock crows on the left and all
Is well .   .   .

. . .

                    . . . not balances
That we achieve but balances that happen,

As a man and woman meet and love forthwith.
Perhaps there are moments of awakening,
Extreme, fortuitous, personal, in which

We more than awaken, sit on the edge of sleep,
As on an elevation, and behold
The academies like structures in a mist.

x

The major abstraction is the idea of man
And major man is its exponent, abler
In the abstract than in his singular,

More fecund as principle than particle,
Happy fecundity, flor-abundant force,
In being more than an exception, part,

Though an heroic part, of the commonal.
The major abstraction is the commonal,
The inanimate, difficult visage . . .

      .   .   .

> [from *Notes Toward*
> *A Supreme Fiction*]

Lines from *It Must Change*

WALLACE STEVENS

iv

Two things of opposite natures seem to depend
On one another, as a man depends
On a woman, day on night, the imagined

On the real. This is the origin of change.
Winter and spring, cold copulars, embrace
And forth the particulars of rapture come.

Music falls on the silence like a sense,
A passion that we feel, not understand.
Morning and afternoon are clasped together

And North and South are an intrinsic couple
And sun and rain a plural, like two lovers
That walk away as one in the greenest body.

.   .   .

In Distrust of Merits

MARIANNE MOORE

Strengthened to live, strengthened to die for
    medals and positioned victories?
They're fighting, fighting, fighting the blind
    man who thinks he sees—
who cannot see that the enslaver is
enslaved; the hater, harmed. O shining O
    firm star, O tumultuous
      ocean lashed till small things go
    as they will, the mountainous
      wave makes us who look, know

depth. Lost at sea before they fought! O
    star of David, star of Bethlehem,
O black imperial lion
    of the Lord—emblem
of a risen world—be joined at last, be
joined. There is hate's crown beneath which all is
    death; there's love's without which none
      is king; the blessed deeds bless
    the halo. As contagion
      of sickness makes sickness,

contagion of trust can make trust. They're
    fighting in deserts and caves, one by
one, in battalions and squadrons;
    they're fighting that I
may yet recover from the disease, My
Self; some have it lightly; some will die. 'Man
      wolf to man'; yes. We devour
        ourselves. The enemy could not
    have made a greater breach in our
      defenses. One pilot–

ing a blind man can escape him, but
    Job disheartened by false comfort knew
that nothing can be so defeating
    as a blind man who
can see. O alive who are dead, who are
proud not to see, O small dust of the earth
      that walks so arrogantly,
        trust begets power and faith is
    an affectionate thing. We
      vow, we make this promise
to the fighting—it's a promise—'We'll
    never hate black, white, red, yellow, Jew,
Gentile, Untouchable.' We are
    not competent to
make our vows. With set jaw they are fighting,
fighting, fighting—some we love whom we know,
    some we love but know not—that
      hearts may feel and not be numb.
    It cures me; or am I what
      I can't believe in? Some

in snow, some on crags, some in quicksands,
    little by little, much by much, they
are fighting fighting fighting that where
    there was death there may
be life. 'When a man is prey to anger,
he is moved by outside things; when he holds

his ground in patience patience
     patience, that is action or
beauty,' the soldier's defense
    and hardest armor for

the fight. The world's an orphans' home. Shall
    we never have peace without sorrow?
without pleas of the dying for
    help that won't come? O
quiet form upon the dust, I cannot
look and yet I must. If these great patient
    dyings—all these agonies
       and woundbearings and bloodshed—
can teach us how to live, these
    dyings were not wasted.

Hate-hardened heart, O heart of iron,
    iron is iron till it is rust.
There never was a war that was
    not inward; I must
fight till I have conquered in myself what
causes war, but I would not believe it.
    I inwardly did nothing.
    O Iscariotlike crime!
    Beauty is everlasting
    and dust is for a time.

Lines from *Avenger, What Wrong?*

JAMES RORTY

The danger, I had thought, lay not in the quarrels, but in the
    weapons. Arrows
Would be preferable to guns, fists to clubs, and best of all,
Words, that break no bones, but harmlessly
Explode themselves in print.

But the words of this Avenger are the venomed hiss of a steel cobra;
Something new in the world, sexless but savage, dead
But deadly, acrid as a zombie's breath, words that extend
The bomber's radius, the crawl and lunge of the armored column.

Teach these steel serpents to breed, and they belch into the world
    clanking the Avenger's speech;
Populate the globe with these machines and their tenders, and lo,
At last the universal language, superseding all others.
The mechanic listens attentively; the sounds of machines and men
Are the symptoms that tell: Are they efficient? Are they morally fit
    to kill? . . .

This is the Avenger's secret weapon, the monstrous
Bastard of man and the machine, the steel cobra beyond good and
    evil.
This is the mutation the lice and the ants
Have been waiting for; like the mule, the sterile variant requiring
The separate propagation of sire and dam. "Something will slip,"
Says an eloquent have-not louse proclaiming. "From despair
The human sire will soon be impotent, and then
Rust, our glorious ally, will consume the dam."

   .   .   .

Glory. Revenge overtakes the Avenger and Justice is done
For lice. The little red teeth of the rust will gnaw
At the eyes, the throat of the steel cobra, sprawled and limp, the
    jaws
Open to recite the conquering words. But the rust
Works soundlessly; only the louse-hum is heard
Louder and louder. The statesmen-lice, the scholars
Burrowing in the ruins of Louvain and the British Museum,
Fighting over dates, are shocked to find their human colleagues lied
So lavishly, the records of the twentieth century
Still smell, despite the purge of flame, the long
Crumble of time and weather.

Always the question: What was the great wrong? What
Was the Avenger avenging?

Putty face, hurt mouth, hating eyes, what wrong?
What slaver of impotence sent you to that
Perverse mating with power? What frantic lust
Jumped the misogenate gap to mount
The apocalyptic iron beast? What shame,
What drooling weakness drove you to this idiot victory?
                              Avenger, what wrong?

[from *The Bridge*]

Lines from *Cape Hatteras*

HART CRANE

Walt, tell me, Walt Whitman, if infinity
Be still the same as when you walked the beach
Near Paumanok—your lone patrol—and heard the
        wraith
Through surf, its bird note there a long time falling . . .
For you, the panoramas and this breed of towers,
Of you—the theme that's statured in the cliff.
O Saunterer on free ways still ahead!
Not this our empire yet, but labyrinth
Wherein your eyes, like the Great Navigator's without ship,
Gleam from the great stones of each prison crypt
Of canyoned traffic . . .   Confronting the Exchange,
Surviving in a world of stocks,—they also range
Across the hills where second timber strays
Back over Connecticut farms, abandoned pastures,—
Sea eyes and tidal, undenying, bright with myth!

The nasal whine of power whips a new universe . . .
Where spouting pillars spoor the evening sky,
Under the looming stacks of the gigantic power house
Stars prick the eyes with sharp ammoniac proverbs,
New verities, new inklings in the velvet hummed
Of dynamos, where hearing's leash is strummed . . .

Power's script,—wound, bobbin-bound, refined—
Is stropped to the slap of belts on booming spools, spurred
Into the bulging bouillon, harnessed jelly of the stars.
Towards what? The forked crash of split thunder parts
Our hearing momentwise; but fast in whirling armatures,
As bright as frogs' eyes, giggling in the girth
Of steely gizzards—axle-bound, confined
In coiled precision, bunched in mutual glee
The bearings glint,—O murmurless and shined
In oilrinsed circles of blind ecstasy!

Lines from *The Descendent and the Id*
(*A Monologue in Regard to Heredity*)
ANNA HEMPSTEAD BRANCH

Once, when the Scholar—in his book, you know,
That talks of Ids and Biophors and so
Makes much rebellious dreaming come and go—

With that great nonchalance of his, my ease
Had interrupted; (Ids! Such things as these!)
I sought myself through earth and fire and seas;

And found it not—but many things beside;
Behemoth old, Leviathans that ride,
And protoplasm, and jellies of the tide.

Then wandering upward through the solid earth
With its dim sounds, potential rage and mirth,
I faced a dim Forefather of my birth,

And thus addressed Him: "All of you that lie
Safe in the dust or ride along the sky—
Lo, these and these and these! But where am I?

.   .   .

"Before the day that brought me forth had found me,
Your subtle raiment wrapped itself around me,
Even when I was not your faint hands had bound me.

"Since thy hands made me—but not fair, not fine!—
Then at the end some piteous look of thine
Must plead forgiveness for these sins of mine."

Thus did I speak, while that poor face arraigned me—
" 'T was thy frail spirit in my heart detained me.
Thy thought, wrought strangely in my own, constrained me."

For when She leaned to Him in the great bliss
(Oh I were wrong to tell their spirits this—)
All my life's sweetness went to make that kiss!

Now, when I beg them, as my hunger must,
Laughing they lay into my hands of trust
The Dead Sea apple that is full of dust.

How they have bruised me! From this soul of mine
Danced out the vintage and drank up the wine.

For when the master bade them in to sup,
Between hot hands they snatched the golden cup,
Lo—I was in it—and they drank me up.

So I was spent, as wind is among sand,
In solemn splendors of the saraband.

Yet I, condemned by them to such vast leisure,
Can laugh to think of that great storm of pleasure,—
Those mad dead feet that danced so wild a measure.

Those pitying eyes! I will not let them see
How I go frail for want of strength in Thee.
I will not make them shed new tears for me.

Poor eyes that looked on love so many years,
Filled with desire thereof—knowing no fears—
Looking through mine are blinded now with tears.

Poor feet, that once tumultuous would go,
Now wistfully in mind must creep so slow,
I could have run too, but ye said me no.

. . .

Rocked in the whirlwind of their son's desires,
Their bosoms blow upon a blast of fires.
Oh, wind of flame that through my melting bone
Blows the white faces of my burning sires.

For they that leave no sons are comforted,
So placidly their downward steps are led
To those vague nations moving in the dust,
Serene, secure, and being dead, are dead!

But these that bore a child shall never be
Delighted with the elements and free.
They make of body and soul their Heaven and Hell,
And they, being dead, shall live again in me.

. . .

"Feast thou, my son"—but ye have eaten the bread!
"Dance thou, my son"—Ye have broken the pipes, I said.
So through my heart in desolate array—
They pass and pass and are uncomforted.

. . .

So of this dual breathing was I made,
Fragile, eternal, wonderful, afraid,
Rapturous, guilty, flaunting and dismayed.

While their thin laughter echoing in my bone
Reminds me that my flesh is not my own.
Hands off, hands off, and let my soul alone!

.   .   .

Oh for some thunder that should rush through me!
Some rain to purge me utterly of Thee,
And leave me naked and small, barren and free.

.   .   .

Then spoke that rapt Philosopher, that bore
The little, restless, splendid Biophor.
"Thou art not, truly. Nay, what wouldst thou more?

.   .   .

"For you that say, with vanity half hid,
'I willed and said and made and had and did'—
Look you, with curious eyes, upon the Id.

.   .   .

"Here is thy will, thy war, thy heavenly fire,
Thy dust, thy want, thy labor, and thy hire,
The Dream, the anger, and the old desire.

"Through this small Id the old barbarians rove,
And ancient hierarchies slowly move—
And kings and clowns and slaves—and hate and love.

"For as the fragile cloud accepts the air
Thy thoughts receive their thoughts, and everywhere
They blow thy dreams about. Thou art not there.

"*What Dream hast thou?*" Then through my soul there came
A light that burned through weariness and shame,
The virginal presence of the clean, first flame.

.   .   .

O fluttering fire! O little pale blue wreath!
O radiant substance, hovering over death!
This, then, is I, made of God's living breath.

.   .   .

Slowly I feel the ancient custom fall
Like shattered rain from off a steady wall,
And great "I will" is stronger than them all.

.   .   .

Last night the old ancestral pageant came,
Bearing the ancient virtue and the shame.
God, in my hand, had written a New Name.

Sonnets

GEORGE SANTAYANA

vii

I would I might forget that I am I,
And break the heavy chain that binds me fast,
Whose links about myself my deeds have cast.
What in the body's tomb doth buried lie
Is boundless; 't is the spirit of the sky,
Lord of the future, guardian of the past,
And soon must forth, to know his own at last.
In his large life to live, I fain would die.
Happy the dumb beast, hungering for food,
But calling not his suffering his own;
Blessèd the angel, gazing on all good,
But knowing not he sits upon a throne;
Wretched the mortal, pondering his mood,
And doomed to know his aching heart alone.

xxv

As in the midst of battle there is room
For thoughts of love, and in foul sin for mirth;
As gossips whisper of a trinket's worth

Spied by the death-bed's flickering candle-gloom;
As in the crevices of Caesar's tomb
The sweet herbs flourish on a little earth:
So in this great disaster of our birth
We can be happy, and forget our doom.
For morning, with a ray of tenderest joy
Gilding the iron heaven, hides the truth,
And evening gently woos us to employ
Our grief in idle catches. Such is youth;
Till from that summer's trance we wake, to find
Despair before us, vanity behind.

Thought's End

LÉONIE ADAMS

I'd watched the hills drink the last color of light,
All shapes grow bright and wane on the pale air,
Till down the traitorous east there came the night,
And swept the circle of my seeing bare;
Its intimate beauty like a wanton's veil
Tore from the void as from an empty face.
I felt at being's rim all being fail,
And my one body pitted against space.
O heart more frightened than a wild bird's wings,
Beating at green, now is no fiery mark,
But heaven empty of accustomed things.
Be self no more against the flooding dark:
There thousandwise sown in that cloudy blot,
Stars that are worlds look out and see you not.

Cruciform
WINIFRED WELLES

Here in the sand, where someone laid him down,
The one known human signature is clear.
Whether woman or man, white-skinned or brown,
Whether the outflung arms were so for fear,
Or agony, or weariness, or shame,
Here, in one line athwart another line,
Is briefly written the one mutual name,
A savior's, or a thief's, or yours, or mine.
Dunes sifted undersea long since have borne
This selfsame cross, small and anonymous.
Tan deserts that the wind has not yet worn
Will print this symbol, and not one of us
But then, or some day, could lie down and fit
Our desolate arms and bodies into it.

Bereft
ROBERT FROST

Where had I heard this wind before
Change like this to a deeper roar?
What would it take my standing there for,
Holding open a restive door,
Looking down hill to a frothy shore?
Summer was past and day was past.
Sombre clouds in the West were massed.
Out in the porch's sagging floor,
Leaves got up in a coil and hissed,
Blindly struck at my knee and missed.
Something sinister in the tone
Told me my secret must be known:

Word I was in the house alone
Somehow must have gotten abroad,
Word I was in my life alone,
Word I had no one left but God.

West-Running Brook

ROBERT FROST

"Fred, where is north?"
           "North? North is there, my love.
The brook runs west."
           "West-running Brook then call it."
(West-running Brook men call it to this day.)
"What does it think it's doing running west
When all the other country brooks flow east
To reach the ocean? It must be the brook
Can trust itself to go by contraries
The way I can with you—and you with me—
Because we're—we're—I don't know what we are.
What are we?"
        "Young or new?"
             "We must be something.
We've said we two. Let's change that to we three.
As you and I are married to each other,
We'll both be married to the brook. We'll build
Our bridge across it, and the bridge shall be
Our arm thrown over it asleep beside it.
Look, look, it's waving to us with a wave
To let us know it hears me."
        "Why, my dear,
That wave's been standing off this jut of shore—"
(The black stream, catching on a sunken rock,
Flung backward on itself in one white wave,
And the white water rode the black forever,

Not gaining but not losing, like a bird
White feathers from the struggle of whose breast
Flecked the dark stream and flecked the darker pool
Below the point, and were at last driven wrinkled
In a white scarf against the far shore alders.)
"That wave's been standing off this jut of shore
Ever since rivers, I was going to say,
Were made in heaven. It was n't waved to us."

"It was n't, yet it was. If not to you
It was to me—in an annunciation."

"Oh, if you take it off to lady-land,
As't were the country of the Amazons
We men must see you to the confines of
And leave you there, ourselves forbid to enter,—
It is your brook! I have no more to say."

"Yes, you have, too. Go on. You thought of something."

"Speaking of contraries, see how the brook
In that white wave runs counter to itself.
It is from that in water we were from
Long, long before we were from any creature.
Here we, in our impatience of the steps,
Get back to the beginning of beginnings,
The stream of everything that runs away.
Some say existence like a Pirouot
And Pirouette, forever in one place,
Stands still and dances, but it runs away,
It seriously, sadly, runs away
To fill the abyss' void with emptiness.
It flows beside us in this water brook,
But it flows over us. It flows between us
To separate us for a panic moment.
It flows between us, over us, and *with* us.
And it is time, strength, tone, light, life and love—
And even substance lapsing unsubstantial;

The universal cataract of death
That spends to nothingness—and unresisted,
Save by some strange resistance in itself,
Not just a swerving, but a throwing back,
As if regret were in it and were sacred.
It has this throwing backward on itself
So that the fall of most of it is always
Raising a little, sending up a little.
Our life runs down in sending up the clock.
The brook runs down in sending up our life.
The sun runs down in sending up the brook.
And there is something sending up the sun.
It is this backward motion toward the source,
Against the stream, that most we see ourselves in,
The tribute of the current to the source.
It is from this in nature we are from.
It is most us."
                    "Today will be the day
You said so."
                    "No, today will be the day
You said the brook was called West-running Brook."

"Today will be the day of what we both said."

Mr. Flood's Party

EDWIN ARLINGTON ROBINSON

Old Eben Flood, climbing alone one night
Over the hill between the town below
And the forsaken upland hermitage
That held as much as he should ever know
On earth again of home, paused warily.
The road was his with not a native near;
And Eben, having leisure, said aloud,
For no man else in Tilbury Town to hear:

"Well, Mr. Flood, we have the harvest moon
Again, and we may not have many more;
The bird is on the wing, the poet says,
And you and I have said it here before.
Drink to the bird." He raised up to the light
The jug that he had gone so far to fill,
And answered huskily: "Well, Mr. Flood,
Since you propose it, I believe I will."

Alone, as if enduring to the end
A valiant armor of scarred hopes outworn,
He stood there in the middle of the road
Like Roland's ghost winding a silent horn.
Below him, in the town among the trees,
Where friends of other days had honored him,
A phantom salutation of the dead
Rang thinly till old Eben's eyes were dim.

Then, as a mother lays her sleeping child
Down tenderly, fearing it may awake,
He set the jug down slowly at his feet
With trembling care, knowing that most things break;
And only when assured that on firm earth
It stood, as the uncertain lives of men
Assuredly did not, he paced away,
And with his hand extended paused again:

"Well, Mr. Flood, we have not met like this
In a long time; and many a change has come
To both of us, I fear, since last it was
We had a drop together. Welcome home!"
Convivially returning with himself,
Again he raised the jug up to the light;
And with an acquiescent quaver said:
"Well, Mr. Flood, if you insist, I might.

"Only a very little, Mr. Flood—
For auld lang syne. No more, sir; that will do."

So, for the time, apparently it did,
And Eben evidently thought so too;
For soon amid the silver loneliness
Of night he lifted up his voice and sang,
Secure, with only two moons listening,
Until the whole harmonious landscape rang—

"For auld lang syne." The weary throat gave out,
The last word wavered; and the song was done.
He raised again the jug regretfully
And shook his head, and was again alone.
There was not much that was ahead of him,
And there was nothing in the town below—
Where strangers would have shut the many doors
That many friends had opened long ago.

Karma

EDWIN ARLINGTON ROBINSON

Christmas was in the air and all was well
With him, but for a few confusing flaws
In divers of God's images. Because
A friend of his would neither buy nor sell,
Was he to answer for the axe that fell?
He pondered; and the reason for it was,
Partly, a slowly freezing Santa Claus
Upon the corner, with his beard and bell.

Acknowledging an improvident surprise,
He magnified a fancy that he wished
The friend whom he had wrecked were here again.
Not sure of that, he found a compromise;
And from the fulness of his heart he fished
A dime for Jesus who had died for men.

From *Octaves*

EDWIN ARLINGTON ROBINSON

i

We thrill too strangely at the master's touch;
We shrink too sadly from the larger self
Which for its own completeness agitates
And undetermines us; we do not feel—
We dare not feel it yet—the splendid shame
Of uncreated failure; we forget,
The while we groan, that God's accomplishment
Is always and unfailingly at hand.

ii

Tumultuously void of a clean scheme
Whereon to build, whereof to formulate,
The legion life that riots in mankind
Goes ever plunging upward, up and down,
Most like some crazy regiment at arms,
Undisciplined of aught but Ignorance,
And ever led resourcelessly along
To brainless carnage by drunk trumpeters.

iii

To me the groaning of world-worshippers
Rings like a lonely music played in hell
By one with art enough to cleave the walls
Of heaven with his cadence, but without
The wisdom or the will to comprehend
The strangeness of his own perversity,
And all without the courage to deny
The profit and the pride of his defeat.

iv

While we are drilled in error, we are lost
Alike to truth and usefulness. We think
We are great warriors now, and we can brag

Like Titans; but the world is growing young,
And we, the fools of time, are growing with it:—
We do not fight to-day, we only die;
We are too proud of death, and too ashamed
Of God, to know enough to be alive.

v

There is one battle-field whereon we fall
Triumphant and unconquered; but, alas!
We are too fleshly fearful of ourselves
To fight there till our days are whirled and blurred
By sorrow, and the ministering wheels
Of anguish take us eastward, where the clouds
Of human gloom are lost against the gleam
That shines on Thought's impenetrable mail.

vi

When we shall hear no more the cradle-songs
Of ages—when the timeless hymns of Love
Defeat them and outsound them—we shall know
The rapture of that large release which all
Right science comprehends; and we shall read,
With unoppressed and unoffended eyes,
That record of All-Soul whereon God writes
In everlasting runes the truth of Him.

vii

The guerdon of new childhood is repose:—
Once he has read the primer of right thought,
A man may claim between two smithy strokes
Beatitude enough to realize
God's parallel completeness in the vague
And incommensurable excellence
That equitably uncreates itself
And makes a whirlwind of the Universe.

viii

There is no loneliness:—no matter where
We go, nor whence we come, nor what good friends

Forsake us in the seeming, we are all
At one with a complete companionship;
And though forlornly joyless be the ways
We travel, the compensate spirit-gleams
Of Wisdom shaft the darkness here and there,
Like scattered lamps in unfrequented streets.

ix

When one that you and I had all but sworn
To be the purest thing God ever made
Bewilders us until at last it seems
An angel has come back restigmatized,—
Faith wavers, and we wonder what there is
On earth to make us faithful any more,
But never are quite wise enough to know
The wisdom that is in that wonderment.

x

Where does a dead man go?—The dead man dies;
But the free life that would no longer feed
On fagots of outburned and shattered flesh
Wakes to a thrilled invisible advance,
Unchained (or fettered else) of memory;
And when the dead man goes it seems to me
'T were better for us all to do away
With weeping, and be glad that he is gone.

xi

Still through the dusk of dead, blank-legended,
And unremunerative years we search
To get where life begins, and still we groan
Because we do not find the living spark
Where no spark ever was; and thus we die,
Still searching, like poor old astronomers
Who totter off to bed and go to sleep,
To dream of untriangulated stars.

xii

With conscious eyes not yet sincere enough
To pierce the glimmered cloud that fluctuates
Between me and the glorifying light
That screens itself with knowledge, I discern
The searching rays of wisdom that reach through
The mist of shame's infirm credulity,
And infinitely wonder if hard words
Like mine have any message for the dead.

xiii

I grant you friendship is a royal thing,
But none shall ever know that royalty
For what it is till he has realized
His best friend in himself. 'T is then, perforce,
That man's unfettered faith indemnifies
Of its own conscious freedom the old shame,
And love's revealed infinitude supplants
Of its own wealth and wisdom the old scorn.

xiv

Though the sick beast infect us, we are fraught
Forever with indissoluble Truth,
Wherein redress reveals itself divine,
Transitional, transcendent. Grief and loss,
Disease and desolation, are the dreams
Of wasted excellence; and every dream
Has in it something of an ageless fact
That flouts deformity and laughs at years.

xviii

Like a white wall whereon forever breaks
Unsatisfied the tumult of green seas,
Man's unconjectured godliness rebukes
With its imperial silence the lost waves
Of insufficient grief. This mortal surge
That beats against us now is nothing else

Than plangent ignorance. Truth neither shakes
Nor wavers; but the world shakes, and we shriek.

xix
Nor jewelled phrase nor mere mellifluous rhyme
Reverberates aright, or ever shall,
One cadence of that infinite plain-song
Which is itself all music. Stronger notes
Than any that have ever touched the world
Must ring to tell it—ring like hammer-blows,
Right-echoed of a chime primordial,
On anvils, in the gleaming of God's forge.

xxii
Forebodings are the fiends of Recreance;
The master of the moment, the clean seer
Of ages, too securely scans what is,
Ever to be appalled at what is not;
He sees beyond the groaning borough lines
Of Hell, God's highways gleaming, and he knows
That Love's complete communion is the end
Of anguish to the liberated man.

xxiii
Here by the windy docks I stand alone,
But yet companioned. There the vessel goes,
And there my friend goes with it; but the wake
That melts and ebbs between that friend and me
Love's earnest is of Life's all-purposeful
And all-triumphant sailing, when the ships
Of Wisdom loose their fretful chains and swing
Forever from the crumbled wharves of Time.

Two Sonnets

EDWIN ARLINGTON ROBINSON

ii

Never until our souls are strong enough
To plunge into the crater of the Scheme—
Triumphant in the flash there to redeem
Love's handsel and forevermore to slough,
Like cerements at a played-out masque, the rough
And reptile skins of us whereon we set
The stigma of scared years—are we to get
Where atoms and the ages are one stuff.

Nor ever shall we know the cursed waste
Of life in the beneficence divine
Of starlight and of sunlight and soul-shine
That we have squandered in sin's fail distress,
Till we have drunk, and trembled at the taste,
The mead of Thought's prophetic endlessness.

❀ DEATH

EDNA ST. VINCENT MILLAY / *The Buck in the Snow* / *Sonnets xxxvii and xliv*

ROBINSON JEFFERS / Lines from *Cawdor* / *Night*

EDWIN ARLINGTON ROBINSON / *Two Sonnets, I*

EDGAR LEE MASTERS / Lines from *Epitaph for Us*

WINIFRED WELLES / *Notes on the Mystery* / *The Shape of Memory* / *Torch*

SARA TEASDALE / *Longing*

JAMES RORTY / *Air Burial*

CHARD POWERS SMITH / *Sonnets xxiv and xxv*

※ *These fourteen selections represent a progression among the* poets in their interpretations of death. In Millay's *The Buck in the Snow* there is no interpretation, merely the simple astonishment of life before the fact of death. In the two sonnets she goes a little farther, first into pity, then into romantic incredulity and the possibility of hope.

Jeffers's sensitive account of the disintegration of the brain states poetically the common materialistic notion of death as annihilation, the lapse into the void. In *Night* he celebrates this same void as both primordial and ultimate reality.

In the first of *Two Sonnets*, the second having been given in the previous section, Robinson merely dismisses the idea of an anthropomorphic after-life and affirms, though without mystical finality, some kind of "lone-faring" immortality.

Masters's poem, based in the familiar epitaph, makes explicit the doctrine of maya that is implicit in Jeffers's *Night*. Masters affirms —for the most part in versified prose—that the material world is illusion, and he adds that the nature of Being, into which the dead are received, is Thought. Thus he confirms Holden's perception in *The Poet*, in the section on "Beauty," and Robinson's in the second of *Two Sonnets* previously quoted.

In the three poems given here, Winifred Welles presents three moods in contemplation of the fact of death. In *Notes on the Mystery* she addresses, appalled, the possibility that the old myth of another and heavenly life might be true. In *The Shape of Memory* she raises the suspicion that in some delicate and impalpable way the dead may continue in communication with those who loved them. In *Torch* she suggests that with the annihilation of the body the personality may be absorbed in the "light" which first made the body visible and is itself eternal.

In *Longing*, Sara Teasdale laments the passing of the body, and takes spiritual immortality for granted. In *Air Burial*, Rorty makes the same assumption, leading romantic aspiration into immortality.

My two sonnets go a step farther into arbitrary affirmation of specific, individual immortality, though based in personal assertion rather than mystical revelation. Generally, the elegiac series from which these are taken is overloaded with subjective emotion and rhetoric. Yet I believe that at least these two speak in the cosmic landscape which is one of the qualifications of greatness.

In this section there might well be included a passage from Eliot's *Little Gidding* with its great, chanted—though not often poetic—affirmation of immortality, its prophecy that death is the beginning. If it were possible to excerpt from this poem, it would belong here.

The Buck in the Snow

EDNA ST. VINCENT MILLAY

White sky, over the hemlocks bowed with snow,
Saw you not at the beginning of evening the antlered buck and his
    doe
Standing in the apple orchard? I saw them. I saw them suddenly go,
Tails us, with long leaps lovely and slow,
Over the stone-wall into the wood of hemlocks bowed with snow.

Now lies he here, his wild blood scalding the snow.

How strange a thing is death, bringing to his knees, bringing to his
    antlers
The buck in the snow.
How strange a thing,—a mile away by now, it may be,
Under the heavy hemlocks that as the moments pass
Shift their loads a little, letting fall a feather of snow—
Life, looking out attentive from the eyes of the doe.

Sonnets

EDNA ST. VINCENT MILLAY

xxxvii

Your face is like a chamber where a king
Dies of his wounds, untended and alone,
Stifling with courteous gesture the crude moan
That speaks too loud of mortal perishing,
Rising on elbow in the dark to sing
Some rhyme now out of season but well known
In days when banners in his face were blown
And every woman had a rose to fling.
I know that through your eyes which look on me
Who stand regarding you with pitiful breath,
You see beyond the moment's pause, you see
The sunny sky, the skimming bird beneath,
And, fronting on your windows hopelessly,
Black in the noon, the broad estates of Death.

xliv

How healthily their feet upon the floor
Strike down! These are no spirits, but a band
Of children, surely, leaping hand in hand
Into the air in groups of three and four,
Wearing their silken rags as if they wore
Leaves only and light grasses, or a strand
Of black elusive seaweed oozing sand,
And running hard as if along a shore.
I know how lost forever, and at length
How still these lovely tossing limbs shall lie,
And the bright laughter and the panting breath;
And yet, before such beauty and such strength,
Once more, as always when the dance is high,
I am rebuked that I believe in death.

Lines from *Cawdor*

ROBINSON JEFFERS

Who lay under the sheer below them, his broken shoulders
Bulging his coat in lumps the starlight regarded.
The bone vessel where all the nerves had met
For counsel while they were living, and the acts and thoughts
Been formed, was burst open, its gray and white jellies
Flung on the stones like liquor from a broken flask,
Mixed with some streamers of blood.

        The vivid consciousness
That waking or dreaming, its twenty years, infallibly
Felt itself unitary, was now divided:
Like the dispersion of a broken hive: the brain-cells
And rent fragments of cells finding
After their communal festival of life particular deaths.
In their deaths they dreamed a moment, the unspent chemistry
Of life resolving its powers; some in the cold star-gleam
Some in the cooling darkness in the crushed skull.

But shine and shade were indifferent to them, their dreams
Determined by temperatures, access of air,
Wetness or drying, as the work of the autolytic
Enzymes of the last hunger hasted or failed.

Yet there appeared, whether by chance or whether
From causes in their common origin and recent union,
A rhythmic sympathy among the particular dreams.
A wave of many minute delicious enjoyments
Would travel across the spilth; then a sad fading
Would follow it, a wave of infinitesimal pains,
And a pause, and the pleasures again. These waves both lessened
In power and slowed in time; the fragments of consciousness
Beginning to lapse out of the frailties of life
And enter another condition. The strained peace
Of the rock has no repose, it is wild and shuddering, it travels

In the teeth of locked strains unimaginable paths;
It is full of desire; but the brittle iniquities of pleasure
And pain are not there. These fragments now approached
What they would enter in a moment, the peace of the earth.

Night

ROBINSON JEFFERS

The ebb slips from the rock, the sunken
Tide-rocks lift streaming shoulders
Out of the slack, the slow west
Sombering its torch; a ship's light
Shows faintly, far out,
Over the weight of the prone ocean
On the low cloud.

Over the dark mountain, over the dark pinewood,
Down the long dark valley along the shrunken river,
Returns the splendor without rays, the shining of shadow,
Peace-bringer, the matrix of all shining and quieter of shining.
Where the shore widens on the bay she opens dark wings
And the ocean accepts her glory. O soul worshipful of her
You like the ocean have grave depths where she dwells always,
And the film of waves above that takes the sun takes also
Her, with more love. The sun-lovers have a blond favorite,
A father of lights and noises, wars, weeping and laughter,
Hot labor, lust and delight and the other blemishes.
     Quietness
Flows from her deeper fountain; and he will die; and she is immor-
     tal.

Far off from here the slender
Flocks of the mountain forest
Move among stems like towers

Of the old redwoods to the stream,
No twig crackling; dip shy
Wild muzzles into the mountain water
Among the dark ferns.

O passionately at peace you being secure will pardon
The blasphemies of glowworms, the lamp in my tower, the fretful-
        ness
Of cities, the crescents of the planets, the pride of the stars.
This August night in a rift of cloud Antares reddens,
The great one, the ancient torch, a lord among lost children,
The earth's orbit doubled would not girdle his greatness, one fire
Globed, out of grasp of the mind enormous; but to you O Night
What? Not a spark? What flicker of a spark in the faint far glim-
        mer
Of a lost fire dying in the desert, dim coals of a sand-pit the Be-
        douins
Wandered from at dawn . . .   Ah singing prayer to what
        gulfs tempted
Suddenly are you more lost? To us the near-hand mountain
Be a measure of height, the tide-worn cliff at the sea-gate a measure
        of continuance.

The tide, moving the night's
Vastness with lonely voices,
Turns, the deep dark-shining
Pacific leans on the land,
Feeling his cold strength
To the outmost margins: you Night will resume
The stars in your time.

O passionately at peace when will that tide draw shoreward?
Truly the spouting fountains of light, Antares, Arcturus,
Tire of their flow, they sing one song but they think silence.
The striding winter giant Orion shines, and dreams darkness.
And life, the flicker of men and moths and the wolf on the hill,
Though furious for continuance, passionately feeding, passionately
Remaking itself upon its mates, remembers deep inward

The calm mother, the quietness of the womb and the egg,
The primal and the latter silences: dear Night it is memory
Prophesies, prophecy that remembers, the charm of the dark.
And I and my people, we are willing to love the four-score years
Heartily; but as a sailor loves the sea, when the helm is for harbor.

Have men's minds changed,
Or the rock hidden in the deep of the waters of the soul
Broken the surface? A few centuries
Gone by, was none dared not to people
The darkness beyond the stars with harps and habitations.
But now, dear is the truth. Life is grown sweeter and lonelier,
And death is no evil.

Two Sonnets

EDWIN ARLINGTON ROBINSON

i

Just as I wonder at the twofold screen
Of twisted innocence that you would plait
For eyes that uncourageously await
The coming of a kingdom that has been,
So I do wonder what God's love can mean
To you that all so strangely estimate
The purpose and the consequent estate
Of one short shuddering step to the Unseen.

No, I have not your backward faith to shrink
Lone-faring from the doorway of God's home
To find Him in the names of buried men;
Nor your ingenious recreance to think
We cherish, in the life that is to come,
The scattered features of dead friends again.

Lines from *Epitaph for Us*

EDGAR LEE MASTERS

One with the turf, one with the tree
As we are now, you soon shall be,
As you are now, so once were we.

. . .

We are with nature, we have grown
At one with water, earth, and stone—
Man only is separate and alone,

Earth sundered, left to dream and feel
Illusion still in pain made real,
The hope a mist, but fire the wheel.

But what was love, and what was lust,
Memory, passion, pain or trust,
Returned to clay and blown in dust,

Is nature without memory—
Yet as you are, so once were we,
As we are now, you soon shall be,

Blind fellows of the indifferent stars
Healed of your bruises, of your scars
In love and living, in the wars.

Come to us where the secret lies
Under the riddle of the skies,
Surrender fingers, speech, and eyes.

Sink into nature and become
The mystery that strikes you dumb,
Be clay and end your martyrdom.

Rise up as thought, the secret know.
As passionless as stars bestow
Your glances on the world below,

As a man looks at hand or knee.
What is the turf of you, what the tree?
Earth is a phantom—let it be.

Notes on the Mystery

WINIFRED WELLES

When I am gone and all that I have been
Lies hollow of me, oh, what will be the shape,
The color, of my incredible escape?
In what dimension, not of earth, scarce seen,
Shall I slip forth? All tremulous and lean
In my own outline puckered on the dark?
Or on the air an insignificant spark,
Soundlessly bobbing, gruesome, small, and green?
Or shall I, after all, feel final strength
Move forth upon no eerie fire, nor flee
Within some vapor's gray and raveling length,
But, from behind closed eyes, most calmly see
How from my own small side superbly springs
That figure of the legends with tall wings?

The Shape of Memory
WINIFRED WELLES

Under the dark-veined eyelids is a world
Blue as an iris, exquisitely furled,
The flower-shape of memory, rooted deep
In that black lake beneath the first green sleep.
And, like gold seeds of pollen, people there
Float in the half-lit, nightfall-colored air . . . .
Oh, if in some such dream, unearthly, dim,
One of your dead returns, never to him
Speak out your grief, nor ever call his name,
Lest the closed flower split open into flame,
The waters shake and crack. Lie still, lie still,
And let him drift away, and the flower fill
With silence and sink back beneath the lake.
Weep quietly in your sleep, but do not wake.
Sleeping or waking you can never hold
All he has now become, a grain of gold.
And oh, do not forget the dead would die
Another bitterer death if they should try
To answer a remembered human cry.

Torch
WINIFRED WELLES

I lift my hand against the sun
And count the fingers one by one,
Each is a film of flame that licks
Around the bones as dark as wicks.
O burning body, bright and tall,
Figure of gauze, before you fall,
Beckon your kindred close, and call

Before the mounting moment ends,
Your lovers and your well-loved friends.
Fly to this hand, white moth; blue flower,
Loosen your petals in a shower
To melt upon this breast; be shed
In silver drops upon this head,
Gold cloud; O earth, take time to see
How beautiful and clear can be
Ephemeral mortality,
How gallantly in blessèd light
We gleam before our mutual night.
Look now, for soon where stood frail wing,
Translucent mist, silk blossoming,
And woman with uplifted hand,
Only the light itself shall stand.

Longing

SARA TEASDALE

I am not sorry for my soul
    That it must go unsatisfied,
For it can live a thousand times;
    Eternity is deep and wide.

I am not sorry for my soul,
    But oh, my body that must go
Back to a little drift of dust
    Without the joy it longed to know.

Air Burial

JAMES RORTY

Say not, O earth, they are too many and too loud
Who fling their lives like rockets in the sky,
The young, the beautiful, the proud—
O earth, receive them when they die.
Say to them, "Children, it is late."
Press from their eyes the hate.

These were the farthest blooms upon the tree,
Plucked by the thunder and the careless hail;
Now they are quiet and forever free.
Nor can we follow where they sail
Between the star wane and that clouded dawn
Their compassed hearts are set upon.

Mother, bestow them 'neath your ancient cover,
Safe from the thrust of fear and pain;
Lap them in darkness, say to friend and lover:
"These were brave seed, and they shall bloom again."

Sonnets

CHARD POWERS SMITH

xxiv

If this were all! If one named God should come
To tell me she is dead, and that is all;
That things of beauty moulder where they fall;
That time and ruin build their final home:
If some immortal friend should whisper this
And pass along, I still would take the gall,

Nor eat and drink despairing with St. Paul,
But fight the beasts again at Ephesus.

And when the time is near for me to go,
And the earth's lights are dim, and fiends arrive
To pity me and say, We told you so—
You chased a phantom; I shall know the lie.
There never was a god who walked the sky
Can tell me that my love is not alive.

xxv

Something within me has outgrown the seed
That put up leaves to where the fireflies are.
One firefly loved, and faded to a star,
And my green wistfulness swelled with a greed
To grope beyond the winds of time and speed,
And send escaping leaves beyond the bar
Of changing symbols, swept up in the far
High autumn consequence of fleshly need.

My love has gone from earth. The eyes I yearn
To kiss look from the stars. Sunset and cloud
Clothe her in fire. And when the galaxies burn
To white star corpses, she will sweep from the shroud
Of moonlight into the dark, crying onward the proud
Charge of wild horses that will not return.

✿ MYSTICAL REALIZATION

GEORGE SANTAYANA / *Sonnet iii*

ROBERT FROST / *I Could Give All to Time* / *All Revelation*

EDNA ST. VINCENT MILLAY / *Sonnet xxxiii*

T. S. ELIOT / *The Dry Salvages* (from *Four Quartets*)

EDWIN ARLINGTON ROBINSON / Lines from *Lancelot* /
    Lines from *The Three Taverns* / *A Christmas Sonnet* /
    As It Looked Then

CHRISTOPHER LAFARGE / *Mercy by Night*

✿ *After the assertiveness, sometimes desperate, in some of the* preceding sections of this book, the poems here are quiet ones, records of peace in harbor. The arrangement is in the order of the completeness of that attained peace, moving from self-centered mystical perception through steps of more or less Christian self-loss to a final identification with complete emptiness which is also everything.

Santayana's sonnet is an affirmation of personal inner awareness —which he severally calls "the inward vision," "the soul's invincible surmise," and "faith"—as the condition of mystical union with ultimate reality which, in a vocabulary close to Holden's and Robinson's, he calls "the thought divine." In spite of Santayana's orthodox Christianity, this is no more than a statement of self-realizing pagan mysticism which in fact was the easiest kind for the typical agnostics of the twenties to attain.

In the two poems given here, Frost, though celebrating the ultimate reality of the inner self, identifies that reality with its perception of what is outside itself. Millay goes farther, moving out of the self into pantheistic identification with external Being.

Eliot, always preoccupied with "the point of intersection of the Timeless / With Time," does not proclaim in *The Dry Salvages* that he has attained that point which is "something given / And taken, in a lifetime's death in love," but he states with mystical conviction that the point will be reached "at last." The statement is less complete than the affirmation of immortality in *Little Gidding*, but it is more poetical and mystical and therefore more convincing.

Although Eliot, in the *Four Quartets*, speaks for mankind, yet we can hear the poet speaking and we know that the search is his own. Robinson, on the other hand, usually speaks in dramatic narrative—the *Octaves*, given earlier, is one of the partial exceptions— and the world of people, not the poet, is right with us. The last few pages of *Lancelot* provide, I suppose, the most complete account of inner Christianity in secular literature, the woman attaining her Grace by sending the man away from her to find his. *The Three Taverns*, on the other hand, being a monologue of Paul on his way to be executed in Rome, is a statement of Christian doctrine and mysticism combined, a wonderfully comprehensive poem—and not a very poetic one—cut to a few excerpts here in order to show the sweep of Robinson's Christian understanding.

A Christmas Sonnet carries this understanding to the point of a Christian flavor thrown over Robinson's fundamentally pantheistic mysticism. His *As It Looked Then* envelops man's self and the cosmos in a single moment's perception and returns them, as nearly unsymbolized as expression can be, to the timeless, original and final state of unsymbolized Being. LaFarge, in a supreme profession of metaphysical Christianity, adds a postscript that the condition of unsymbolized Being is Mercy—or Love.

Sonnet

GEORGE SANTAYANA

iii

O world, thou choosest not the better part!
It is not wisdom to be only wise,
And on the inward vision close the eyes,
But it is wisdom to believe the heart.
Columbus found a world, and had no chart,
Save one that faith deciphered in the skies;
To trust the soul's invincible surmise
Was all his science and his only art.
Our knowledge is a torch of smoky pine
That lights the pathway but one step ahead
Across a void of mystery and dread.
Bid, then, the tender light of faith to shine
By which alone the mortal heart is led
Unto the thinking of the thought divine.

I Could Give All to Time

ROBERT FROST

To Time it never seems that he is brave
To set himself against the peaks of snow
To lay them level with the running wave,
Nor is he overjoyed when they lie low,
But only grave, contemplative and grave.

What now is inland shall be ocean isle,
Then eddies playing round a sunken reef
Like the curl at the corner of a smile;
And I could share Time's lack of joy or grief
At such a planetary change of style.

I could give all to Time except—except
What I myself have held. But why declare
The things forbidden that while the Customs slept
I have crossed to Safety with? For I am There,
And what I would not part with I have kept.

All Revelation

ROBERT FROST

A head thrusts in as for the view,
But where it is it thrusts in from
Or what it is it thrusts into
By that Cyb'laean avenue,
And what can of its coming come,

And whither it will be withdrawn,
And what take hence or leave behind,
These things the mind has pondered on

A moment and still asking gone.
Strange apparition of the mind!

But the impervious geode
Was entered, and its inner crust
Of crystals with a ray cathode
At every point and facet glowed
In answer to the mental thrust.

Eyes seeking the response of eyes
Bring out the stars, bring out the flowers,
Thus concentrating earth and skies
So none need be afraid of size.
All revelation has been ours.

Sonnet

E D N A S T. V I N C E N T M I L L A Y

xxxiii

I shall go back again to the bleak shore
And build a little shanty on the sand
In such a way that the extremist band
Of brittle seaweed will escape my door
But by a yard or two; and nevermore
Shall I return to take you by the hand;
I shall be gone to what I understand,
And happier than I ever was before.
The love that stood a moment in your eyes,
The words that lay a moment on your tongue,
Are one with all that in a moment dies,
A little under-said and over-sung.
But I shall find the sullen rocks and skies
Unchanged from what they were when I was young.

The Dry Salvages

T. S. ELIOT

(The Dry Salvages—presumably *les trois sauvages*—is a small
group of rocks, with a beacon, off the N.E. coast of Cape Ann,
Massachusetts. *Salvages* is pronounced to rhyme with *Assuages*.
Groaner: A whistling buoy.)

i

I do not know much about gods; but I think that the river
Is a strong brown god—sullen, untamed and intractable,
Patient to some degree, at first recognised as a frontier;
Useful, untrustworthy, as a conveyor of commerce;
Then only a problem confronting the builder of bridges.
The problem once solved, the brown god is almost forgotten
By the dwellers in cities—ever, however, implacable,
Keeping his seasons and rages, destroyer, reminder
Of what men choose to forget. Unhonoured, unpropitiated
By worshippers of the machine, but waiting, watching and waiting.
His rhythm was present in the nursery bedroom,
In the rank ailanthus of the April dooryard,
In the smell of grapes on the autumn table,
And the evening circle in the winter gaslight.

  The river is within us, the sea is all about us;
The sea is the land's edge also, the granite
Into which it reaches, the beaches where it tosses
Its hints of earlier and other creation:
The starfish, the hermit crab, the whale's backbone;
The pools where it offers to our curiosity
The more delicate algae and the sea anemone.
It tosses up our losses, the torn seine,
The shattered lobsterpot, the broken oar
And the gear of foreign dead men. The sea has many voices,
Many gods and many voices.
                    The salt is on the briar rose,

The fog is in the fir trees.
                              The sea howl
And the sea yelp, are different voices
Often together heard; the whine in the rigging,
The menace and caress of wave that breaks on water,
The distant rote in the granite teeth,
And the wailing warning from the approaching headland
Are all sea voices, and the heaving groaner
Rounded homewards, and the seagull:
And under the oppression of the silent fog
The tolling bell
Measures time not our time, rung by the unhurried
Ground swell, a time
Older than the time of chronometers, older
Than time counted by anxious worried women
Lying awake, calculating the future,
Trying to unweave, unwind, unravel
And piece together the past and the future,
Between midnight and dawn, when the past is all deception,
The future futureless, before the morning watch
When time stops and time is never ending;
And the ground swell, that is and was from the beginning,
Clangs
The bell.

ii
Where is there an end of it, the soundless wailing,
The silent withering of autumn flowers
Dropping their petals and remaining motionless;
Where is there an end to the drifting wreckage,
The prayer of the bone on the beach, the unprayable
Prayer at the calamitous annunciation?

   There is no end, but addition: the trailing
Consequence of further days and hours,
While emotion takes to itself the emotionless
Years of living among the breakage

Of what was believed in as the most reliable—
And therefore the fittest for renunciation.

There is the final addition, the failing
Pride or resentment at failing powers,
The unattached devotion which might pass for devotionless,
In a drifting boat with a slow leakage,
The silent listening to the undeniable
Clamour of the bell of the last annunciation.

Where is the end of them, the fishermen sailing
Into the wind's tail, where the fog cowers?
We cannot think of a time that is oceanless
Or of an ocean not littered with wastage
Or of a future that is not liable
Like the past, to have no destination.

We have to think of them as forever bailing,
Setting and hauling, while the North East lowers
Over shallow banks unchanging and erosionless
Or drawing their money, drying sails at dockage;
Not as making a trip that will be unpayable
For a haul that will not bear examination.

There is no end of it, the voiceless wailing,
No end to the withering of withered flowers,
To the movement of pain that is painless and motionless,
To the drift of the sea and the drifting wreckage,
The bone's prayer to Death its God. Only the hardly, barely prayable
Prayer of the one Annunciation.

It seems, as one becomes older,
That the past has another pattern, and ceases to be a mere sequence—
Or even development: the latter a partial fallacy,
Encouraged by superficial notions of evolution,
Which becomes, in the popular mind, a means of disowning the past.
The moments of happiness—not the sense of well-being,
Fruition, fulfilment, security or affection,

Or even a very good dinner, but the sudden illumination—
We had the experience but missed the meaning,
And approach to the meaning restores the experience
In a different form, beyond any meaning
We can assign to happiness. I have said before
That the past experience revived in the meaning
Is not the experience of one life only
But of many generations—not forgetting
Something that is probably quite ineffable:
The backward look behind the assurance
Of recorded history, the backward half-look
Over the shoulder, towards the primitive terror.
Now, we come to discover that the moments of agony
(Whether, or not, due to misunderstanding,
Having hoped for the wrong things or dreaded the wrong things,
Is not in question) are likewise permanent
With such permanence as time has. We appreciate this better
In the agony of others, nearly experienced,
Involving ourselves, than in our own.
For our own past is covered by the currents of action,
But the torment of others remains an experience
Unqualified, unworn by subsequent attrition.
People change, and smile: but the agony abides.
Time the destroyer is time the preserver,
Like the river with its cargo of dead Negroes, cows and chicken coops,
The bitter apple and the bite in the apple.
And the ragged rock in the restless waters,
Waves wash over it, fogs conceal it;
On a halcyon day it is merely a monument,
In navigable weather it is always a seamark
To lay a course by: but in the sombre season
Or the sudden fury, is what it always was.

iii

I sometimes wonder if that is what Krishna meant—
Among other things—or one way of putting the same thing:
That the future is a faded song, a Royal Rose or a lavender spray
Of wistful regret for those who are not yet here to regret,

Pressed between yellow leaves of a book that has never been opened
And the way up is the way down, the way forward is the way back.
You cannot face it steadily, but this thing is sure,
That time is no healer: the patient is no longer here.
When the train starts, and the passengers are settled
To fruit, periodicals and business letters
(And those who saw them off have left the platform)
Their faces relax from grief into relief,
To the sleepy rhythm of a hundred hours.
Fare forward, travellers! not escaping from the past
Into different lives, or into any future;
You are not the same people who left that station
Or who will arrive at any terminus,
While the narrowing rails slide together behind you;
And on the deck of the drumming liner
Watching the furrow that widens behind you,
You shall not think "the past is finished"
Or "the future is before us."
At nightfall, in the rigging and the aerial,
Is a voice descanting (though not to the ear,
The murmuring shell of time, and not in any language)
"Fare forward, you who think that you are voyaging;
You are not those who saw the harbour
Receding, or those who will disembark.
Here between the hither and the farther shore
While time is withdrawn, consider the future
And the past with an equal mind.
At the moment which is not of action or inaction
You can receive this: 'on whatever sphere of being
The mind of a man may be intent
At the time of death'—that is the one action
(And the time of death is every moment)
Which shall fructify in the lives of others:
And do not think of the fruit of action.
Fare forward.
                    O voyagers, O seamen,
You who come to port, and you whose bodies
Will suffer the trial and judgment of the sea,

Or whatever event, this is your real destination."
So Krishna, as when he admonished Arjuna
On the field of battle.

                              Not fare well,
But fare forward, voyagers.

iv
Lady, whose shrine stands on the promontory,
Pray for all those who are in ships, those
Whose business has to do with fish, and
Those concerned with every lawful traffic
And those who conduct them.

   Repeat a prayer also on behalf of
Women who have seen their sons or husbands
Setting forth, and not returning
Figlia del tuo figlio,
Queen of Heaven.

   Also pray for those who were in ships, and
Ended their voyage on the sand, in the sea's lips
Or in the dark throat which will not reject them
Or wherever cannot reach them the sound of the sea bell's
Perpetual angelus.

v
To communicate with Mars, converse with spirits,
To report the behaviour of the sea monster,
Describe the horoscope, haruspicate or scry,
Observe disease in signatures, evoke
Biography from the wrinkles of the palm
And tragedy from fingers; release omens
By sortilege, or tea leaves, riddle the inevitable
With playing cards, fiddle with pentagrams
Or barbituric acids, or dissect
The recurrent image into pre-conscious terrors—
To explore the womb, or tomb, or dreams; all these are usual
Pastimes and drugs, and features of the press:

And always will be, some of them especially
When there is distress of nations and perplexity
Whether on the shores of Asia, or in the Edgware Road.
Men's curiosity searches past and future
And clings to that dimension. But to apprehend
The point of intersection of the timeless
With time, is an occupation for the saint—
No occupation either, but something given
And taken, in a lifetime's death in love,
Ardour and selflessness and self-surrender.
For most of us, there is only the unattended
Moment, the moment in and out of time,
The distraction fit, lost in a shaft of sunlight,
The wild thyme unseen, or the winter lightning
Or the waterfall, or music heard so deeply
That it is not heard at all, but you are the music
While the music lasts. These are only hints and guesses,
Hints followed by guesses; and the rest
Is prayer, observance, discipline, thought and action.
The hint half guessed, the gift half understood, is Incarnation.
Here the impossible union
Of spheres of existence is actual,
Here the past and future
Are conquered, and reconciled,
Where action were otherwise movement
Of that which is only moved
And has in it no source of movement—
Driven by daemonic, chthonic
Powers. And right action is freedom
From past and future also.
For most of us, this is the aim
Never here to be realised;
Who are only undefeated
Because we have gone on trying;
We, content at the last
If our temporal reversion nourish
(Not too far from the yew-tree)
The life of significant soil.

Lines from *Lancelot*

EDWIN ARLINGTON ROBINSON

Time brought his weary search to a dusty end
One afternoon in Almesbury, where he left,
With a glad sigh, his horse in an innyard;
And while he ate his food and drank his wine,
Thrushes, indifferent in their loyalty
To Arthur dead and to Pan never dead,
Sang as if all were now as all had been.

• • •

                      He found the queen,
But she was not the Queen of white and gold
That he had seen before him for so long.
There was no gold; there was no gold anywhere.
The black hood, and the white face under it,
And the blue frightened eyes, were all he saw—
Until he saw more black, and then more white.
Black was a foreign foe to Guinevere;
And in the glimmering stillness where he found her
Now, it was death; and she Alcestis-like,
Had waited unaware for the one hand
Availing, so he thought, that would have torn
Off and away the last fell shred of doom
That was destroying and dishonoring
All the world held of beauty. His eyes burned
With a sad anger as he gazed at hers
That shone with a sad pity. "No," she said;
"You have not come for this. We are done with this.
For there are no queens here; there is a Mother.
The Queen that was is only a child now,
And you are strong. Remember you are strong,
And that your fingers hurt when they forget
How strong they are."
                   He let her go from him
And while he gazed around him, he frowned hard

And long at the cold walls: "Is this the end
Of Arthur's kingdom and of Camelot?"—
She told him with a motion of her shoulders
All that she knew of Camelot or of kingdoms;
And then said: "We are told of other States
Where there are palaces, if we should need them,
That are not made with hands. I thought you knew."

Dumb, like a man twice banished, Lancelot
Stood gazing down upon the cold stone floor;
And she, demurely, with a calm regard
That he met once and parried, stood apart,
Appraising him with eyes that were no longer
Those he had seen when first they had seen his.
They were kind eyes, but they were not the eyes
Of his desire; and they were not the eyes
That he had followed all the way from Dover.
"I feared the Light was leading you," she said.
"So far by now from any place like this
That I should have your memory, but no more.
Might not that way have been the wiser way?
There is no Arthur now, no Modred now,—
No Guinevere." She paused, and her voice wandered
Away from her own name: "There is nothing now
That I can see between you and the Light
That I have dimmed so long. If you forgive me,
And I believe you do—though I know all
That I have cost, when I was worth so little—
There is no hazard that I see between you
And all you sought so long, and would have found
Had I not always hindered you. Forgive me—
I could not let you go. God pity men
When women love too much—and women more."
He scowled and with an iron shrug he said:
"Yes, there is that between me and the light."
He glared at her black hood as if to seize it;
Their eyes met, and she smiled: "No, Lancelot;
We are going by two roads to the same end;

Or let us hope, at least, what knowledge hides,
And so believe it. We are going somewhere.
Why the new world is not for you and me,
I cannot say; but only one was ours.
I think we must have lived in our one world
All that earth had for us. You are good to me,
Coming to find me here for the last time;
For I should have been lonely many a night,
Not knowing if you cared. I do know now;
And there is not much else for me to know
That earth may tell me. I found in the Tower,
With Modred watching me, that all you said
That rainy night was true. There was time there
To find out everything. There were long days,
And there were nights that I should not have said
God would have made a woman to endure.
I wonder if a woman lives who knows
All she may do."

              "I wonder if one woman
Knows one thing she may do," Lancelot said,
With a sad passion shining out of him
While he gazed on her beauty, palled with black
That hurt him like a sword. The full blue eyes
And the white face were there, and the red lips
Were there, but there was no gold anywhere.
"What have you done with your gold hair?" he said;
"I saw it shining all the way from Dover,
But here I do not see it. Shall I see it?"—
Faintly again she smiled: "Yes, you may see it
All the way back to Dover; but not here.
There's not much of it here, and what there is
Is not for you to see."

              "Well, if not here,"
He said at last, in a low voice that shook,
"Is there no other place left in the world?"

"There is not even the world left, Lancelot,
For you and me."

    "There is France left," he said.
His face flushed like a boy's, but he stood firm
As a peak in the sea and waited.

    "How many lives
Must a man have in one to make him happy?"
She asked, with a wan smile of recollection
That only made the black that was around
Her calm face more funereal: "Was it you,
Or was it Gawaine who said once to me,
'We cannot make one world of two, nor may we
Count one life more than one.' "

.   .   .

    "We are done, you and I,
With what we were. 'Could we go back again,
The fruit that we should find'—but you know best
What we should find. . . . .
. . . . When you see one woman—
When you see me—before you in your fancy,
See me all white and gold, as I was once.
I shall not harm you then; I shall not come
Between you and the Gleam that you must follow,
Whether you will or not. There is no place
For me but where I am; there is no place
For you save where it is that you are going.
If I knew everything as I know that,
I should know more than Merlin, who knew all,
And long ago, that we are to know now.

.   .   .

For me there was no dark until it came
When the King came, and with his heavy shadow
Put out the sun that you made shine again

Before I was to die. So I forgive
The faggots; I can do no more than that—
For you, or God." She looked away from him
And in the casement saw the sunshine dying:
"The time that we have left will soon be gone;
When the bell rings, it rings for you to go,
But not for me to go. It rings for me
To stay—and pray. I, who have not prayed much,
May as well pray now. I have not what you have
To make me see, though I shall have, sometime,
A new light of my own. I saw in the Tower,
When all was darkest and I may have dreamed,
A light that gave to men the eyes of Time
To read themselves in silence. Then it faded,
And the men faded. I was there alone.
I shall not have what you have, or much else—
In this place. I shall see in other places
What is not here. I shall not be alone.
And I shall tell myself that you are seeing
All that I cannot see. For the time now,
What most I see is that I had no choice,
And that you came to me. How many years
Of purgatory shall I pay God for saying
This to you here?" Her words came slowly out,
And her mouth shook.

                  He took her two small hands
That were so pale and empty, and so cold:
"Poor child, I said too much and heard too little
Of what I said. But when I found you here,
So different, so alone, I would have given
My soul to be a chattel and a gage
For dicing fiends to play for, could so doing
Have brought one summer back."

                         "When they are gone,"
She said, with grateful sadness in her eyes,
"We do not bring them back, or buy them back,
Even with our souls. I see now it is best
We do not buy them back, even with our souls."

A slow and hollow bell began to sound
Somewhere above them, and the world became
For Lancelot one wan face—Guinevere's face.
"When the bell rings, it rings for you to go,"
She said; "and you are going . . . I am not.
Think of me always as I used to be,
All white and gold—for that was what you called me.
You may see gold again when you are gone;
And I shall not be there."—He drew her nearer
To kiss the quivering lips that were before him
For the last time. "No, not again," she said;
"I might forget that I am not alone . . .
I shall not see you in this world again,
But I am not alone. No, . . . not alone.
We have had all there was, and you were kind—
Even when you tried so hard once to be cruel.
I knew it then . . . or now I do. Good-bye."
He crushed her cold white hands and saw them falling
Away from him like flowers into a grave.
When she looked up to see him, he was gone;
And that was all she saw till she awoke
In her white cell, where the nuns carried her
With many tears and many whisperings.
"She was the Queen, and he was Lancelot,"
One said. "They were great lovers. It is not good
To know too much of love. We who love God
Alone are happiest. Is it not so, Mother?"—
"We who love God alone, my child, are safest,"
The Mother replied; "and we are not all safe
Until we are all dead. We watch, and pray."

Outside again, Lancelot heard the sound
Of reapers he had seen. With lighter tread
He walked away to them to see them nearer;
He walked and heard again the sound of thrushes
Far off. He saw below him, stilled with yellow,
A world that was not Arthur's, and he saw
The convent roof; and then he could see nothing

But a wan face and two dim lonely hands
That he had left behind. They were down there,
Somewhere, her poor white face and hands, alone.
"No man was ever alone like that," he thought,
Not knowing what last havoc pity and love
Had still to wreak on wisdom. Gradually,
In one long wave it whelmed him, and then broke—
Leaving him like a lone man on a reef,
Staring for what had been with him, but now
Was gone and was a white face under the sea,
Alive there, and alone—always alone.
He closed his eyes, and the white face was there,
But not the gold. The gold would not come back.
There were gold fields of corn that lay around him,
But they were not the gold of Guinevere—
Though men had once, for sake of saying words,
Prattled of corn about it. The still face
Was there, and the blue eyes that looked at him
Through all the stillness of all distances;
And he could see her lips, trying to say
Again, "I am not alone." And that
Was all his life had said to him that he remembered
While he sat there with his hands over his eyes,
And his heart aching. When he rose again
The reapers had gone home. Over the land
Around him in the twilight there was rest.
There was rest everywhere; and there was none
That found his heart. "Why should I look for peace
When I have made the world a ruin of war?"
He muttered; and a Voice within him said:
"Where the Light falls, death falls; a world has died
For you, that a world may live. There is no peace.
Be glad no man or woman bears for ever
The burden of first days. There is no peace."

A word stronger than his willed him away
From Almesbury. All alone he rode that night,
Under the stars, led by the living Voice

That would not give him peace. Into the dark
He rode, but not for Dover. Under the stars,
Alone, all night he rode, out of a world
That was not his, or the King's; and in the night
He felt a burden lifted as he rode,
While he prayed he might bear it for the sake
Of a still face before him that was fading,
Away in a white loneliness. He made,
Once, with a groping hand as if to touch it,
But a black branch of leaves was all he found.

Now the still face was dimmer than before,
And it was not so near him. He gazed hard,
But through his tears he could not see it now;
And when the tears were gone he could see only
That all he saw was fading, always fading;
And she was there alone. She was the world
That he was losing; and the world he sought
Was all a tale for those who had been living,
And had not lived. Once even he turned his horse,
And would have brought his army back with him
To make her free. They should be free together.
But the Voice within him said: "You are not free.
You have come to the world's end, and it is best
You are not free. Where the Light falls, death falls;
And in the darkness comes the Light." He turned
Again; and he rode on, under the stars,
Out of the world, into he knew not what,
Until a vision chilled him and he saw,
Now as in Camelot, long ago in the garden,
The face of Galahad who had seen and died,
And was alive, now in a mist of gold.
He rode on into the dark, under the stars,
And there were no more faces. There was nothing.
But always in the darkness he rode on,
Alone; and in the darkness came the Light.

Lines from *The Three Taverns*

EDWIN ARLINGTON ROBINSON

But I say only, now, that I am Paul—
A prisoner of the Law, and of the Lord
A voice made free. . . . .
. . . . I go now to Rome,
Where Caesar waits for me . . . . .
. . . . The cup that I shall drink
Is mine to drink—the moment or the place
Not mine to say.

    . . .

Once I had said the ways of God were dark,
Meaning by that the dark ways of the Law.
Such is the Glory of our tribulations;
For the Law kills the flesh that kills the Law,
And we are then alive . . . . . .
. . . . The fire that smites
A few on highways, changing all at once,
Is not for all. The power that holds the world
Away from God that holds himself away—
Farther away than all your works and words
Are like to fly without the wings of faith—
Was not, nor ever shall be, a small hazard
Enlivening the ways of easy leisure
Or the cold road of knowledge. When our eyes
Have wisdom, we see more than we remember
. . . . Before we see,
Meanwhile we suffer; and I come to you,
At last, through many storms and through much night.

    . . .

        There be none that shall indite
So much of nothing as the man of words
Who writes in the Lord's name for his name's sake

And has not in his blood the fire of time
To warm eternity.

  •   •   •

The Kingdom is within us, we are told;
And when I say to you that we possess it
In such a measure as faith makes it ours,
I say it with a sinner's privilege
Of having seen and heard, and seen again,
After a darkness; and if I affirm
To the last hour that faith affords alone
The Kingdom entrance and an entertainment,
I do not see myself as one who says
To man that he shall sit with folded hands
Against the Coming.

  •   •   •

                      What is dark
Is dark, and we may not say otherwise;
Yet what may be as dark as a lost fire
For one of us, may still be for another
A coming gleam across the gulf of ages,
And a way home from shipwreck to the shore;
And so, through pangs and ills and desperations,
There may be light for all. There shall be light.
As much as that, you know. You cannot say
This woman or that man will be the next
On whom it falls.

  •   •   •

                Beware of stoics,
And give your left hand to grammarians.

  •   •   •

The best of life, until we see beyond
The shadows of ourselves (and they are less
Than even the blindest of indignant eyes
Would have them) is in what we do not know.

·   ·   ·

                              Many that hate
Their kind are soon to know that without love
Their faith is but the perjured name of nothing.
· · · · · · · · · · I that have lost all else
For wisdom, and the wealth of it, say now
To you that out of wisdom has come love,
That measures and is of itself the measure
Of works and hope and faith.   ·   ·   ·   ·
· · · · · · · · And the last days
Are on the way that you prepare for them,
And was prepared for you, here in a world
Where you have sinned and suffered, striven and seen.

A Christmas Sonnet

EDWIN ARLINGTON ROBINSON

While you that in your sorrow disavow
Service and hope, see love and brotherhood
Far off as ever, it will do no good
For you to wear his thorns upon your brow
For doubt of him. And should you question how
To serve him best, he might say, if he could,
"Whether or not the cross was made of wood
Whereon you nailed me, is no matter now."

Though other saviors have in older lore
A Legend, and for older gods have died—
Though death may wear the crown it always wore
And ignorance be still the sword of pride—
Something is here that was not here before,
And strangely has not yet been crucified.

As It Looked Then
EDWIN ARLINGTON ROBINSON

In a sick shade of spruce, moss-webbed, rock-fed,
Where, long unfollowed by sagacious man,
A scrub that once had been a pathway ran
Blindly from nowhere and to nowhere led,
One might as well have been among the dead
As half way there alive; so I began
Like a malingering pioneer to plan
A vain return—with one last look ahead.

And it was then that like a spoken word
Where there was none to speak, insensibly
A flash of blue that might have been a bird
Grew soon to the calm wonder of the sea—
Calm as a quiet sky that looked to be
Arching a world where nothing had occurred.

Mercy by Night
CHRISTOPHER LA FARGE

Now with a cloud-broom sweep, of lacéd pattern,
Chases of night, brushing asunder
Dutiful stars. Make larger, generous
Moors of darkness. O never mercy may
Creep through such stickling, orderly
Star-sharpness winding!

Then are dispensed with moons, annular Saturn;
Jupiter vanished, Vega gone under;
Redness of Mars fled with red Sirius;
Delivered of Venus; Pleiades, Milky Way,

Pole Star and whirling Nebulae
Swept into blind-rows.

So from the vast of night's regions of darkness,
Looming of vision, as the broom's thunder
Stills from the sharp lightning of starry dust.
Now from an unmooned nothingness survey
On moveless night-moors: mercy,
No orbit binding.

❀ BIBLIOGRAPHY

Léonie Adams, *Poems: A Selection*. Funk & Wagnalls, 1954.

Conrad Aiken, *Collected Poems*. Oxford University Press, 1953.

Stephen Vincent Benét, *John Brown's Body*. Holt, Rinehart & Winston, 1928.

William Rose Benét, *Man Possessed*. George H. Doran, 1927.

Anna Hempstead Branch, *The Shoes That Danced*. Houghton, Mifflin, 1905.

Hart Crane, *Complete Poems & Selected Letters & Prose*. Liveright, 1966.

E. E. Cummings, *Poems 1923-1954*. Harcourt, Brace & World, 1954.

Donald Davidson, *Poems 1922-1961*. University of Minnesota Press, 1966.

Babette Deutsch, *Epistle To Prometheus*. Jonathan Cape & Harrison Smith, 1931.

T. S. Eliot, *Four Quartets*. Harcourt, Brace & World, 1943.

Hildegarde Flanner, *If There Is Time*. New Directions, 1942.

John Gould Fletcher, *Selected Poems*. Farrar & Rinehart, 1938.

Robert Frost, *The Complete Poems Of Robert Frost*. Holt, Rinehart, & Winston, 1949.

Horace Gregory, *Collected Poems*. Holt, Rinehart, & Winston, 1964.

——— *Poems 1930-1940*. Harcourt, Brace, 1941.

Raymond Holden, *Selected Poems*. Henry Holt, 1946.

Robinson Jeffers, *Cawdor & Other Poems*. Random House, 1928.

——— *Selected Poetry Of Robinson Jeffers*. Random House, 1938.

Christopher La Farge, *Poems & Portraits*. Coward, McCann, 1940.

Amy Lowell, *Complete Poetical Works*. Houghton, Mifflin, 1955.

Archibald MacLeish, *Collected Poems*. Houghton Mifflin, 1952.

Edgar Lee Masters, *Toward the Gulf*. Macmillan, 1918.

——— *Starved Rock*. Macmillan, 1919.

Edna St. Vincent Millay, *Collected Poems*. Harper & Row, 1956.

Marianne Moore, *Collected Poems*. Macmillan, 1951.

Edwin Arlington Robinson, *Collected Poems*. Macmillan, 1944.

George Santayana, *Poems*. Scribner's, 1923.

Chard Powers Smith, *Along The Wind*. Yale University Press, 1925.

——— *Prelude To Man*. Peter Pauper Press, 1936.

Wallace Stevens, *Collected Poems*. Knopf, 1954.

Sara Teasdale, *Collected Poems*. Macmillan, 1937.

Mark Van Doren, *Collected & New Poems 1924-1963*. Hill & Wang, 1963.

Sylvia Townsend Warner, *The Espalier*. Chatto & Windus, Ltd. 1925.

Winifred Welles, *The Shape Of Memory*. Henry Holt, 1944.

William Carlos Williams, *The Collected Earlier Poems Of William Carlos Williams*. New Directions, 1951.

Elinor Wylie, *Collected Poems*. Knopf, 1932.